Praise for Thomas H. Lee, MD and
HEALTHCARE'S PATH FORWARD

This book is bold and a must-read for everyone who works in or is passionate about healthcare. Dr. Lee connects lessons learned from the pandemic as a stress test for American healthcare with actionable advice for creating systems that better serve people. His insights on the power of listening and his road map to rebuilding trust are thought provoking. This is an invaluable guide to creating a high-reliability organization, no matter what.

—TINA FREESE DECKER, MHA, MSIE, FACHE,
President and CEO of Corewell Health

As unprecedented challenges confront the future of health delivery, we should be optimistic about the future. *Healthcare's Path Forward* validates that we are prepared, and our strength comes from our core principles (or values). Caregivers and organizations are resilient, adaptive, and innovative, and Tom Lee's book confirms that we are ready for the work ahead.

—JAMES MERLINO, MD, Chief Clinical
Transformation Officer of Cleveland Clinic

"This time is different" is rarely true, and the capacity to sort signal from noise is invaluable for leaders. Dr. Lee shows us what really has changed in our post-Covid healthcare economy: the need for reliability, the primacy of value, and a very human call for authenticity in how we lead teams and care for patients.

—GRIFFIN MYERS, MD, Cofounder and Chief
Medical Officer of Oak Street Health

Tom Lee once again delivers a concise treatise that makes us rethink and reevaluate what we are here to do in our healthcare roles, and how we can better meet the expectations of those who count on us. With the acceleration of crises pushing healthcare providers to the limit and with a spotlight on a long history of healthcare inequity, we must push ourselves to live the values of our organizations routinely and do better on behalf of both our patients and colleagues. That means an unemotional evaluation of what we do and how we do it, and then using trust to speed the change required to alleviate the suffering of our patients. No matter what, we must push for high reliability—for every patient, for every colleague, for every family member and loved one, without excuse. Meaning well was never enough, and this book will hopefully inspire us to *do* well ... or at least better.

—DAVID LUBARSKY, MD, MBA, CEO of UC Davis Health
and Vice Chancellor of Human Health Sciences

Tom Lee sets a course for healthcare organizations to adapt to a quickly evolving landscape centered on trust and a strong culture, where patients behave more like consumers seeking a high-value experience. His call for a shift from incremental change to transformative change serves as inspiration for all those working to improve the system. If our path forward can be one of excellence, trust, respect, inclusion, resilience, and reliability, we will all benefit.

—JAEWON RYU, MD, JD, President and CEO of Geisinger

HEALTHCARE'S
PATH FORWARD

1/1/23

To Adrienne Boissy —

With affection and respect, and high hopes for our collective impact.

Best wishes from

Tom Lee

HEALTHCARE'S
PATH FORWARD

HOW ONGOING CRISES ARE CREATING NEW STANDARDS FOR EXCELLENCE

THOMAS H. LEE, MD

NEW YORK CHICAGO SAN FRANCISCO ATHENS LONDON MADRID
MEXICO CITY MILAN NEW DELHI SINGAPORE SYDNEY TORONTO

1 2 3 4 5 6 7 8 9   LCR   27 26 25 24 23 22

ISBN: 978-1-264-94125-4
MHID: 1-264-94125-0

e-ISBN: 978-1-264-94240-4
e-MHID: 1-264-94240-0

Design by Mauna Eichner and Lee Fukui

Library of Congress Cataloging-in-Publication Data

Names: Lee, Thomas H., author.
Title: Healthcare's path forward : how ongoing crises are creating new
    standards for excellence / Thomas H. Lee.
Description: New York : McGraw Hill, [2023] | Includes bibliographical
    references and index.
Identifiers: LCCN 2022033878 (print) | LCCN 2022033879 (ebook) | ISBN
    9781264941254 (hardback) | ISBN 9781264942404 (ebook)
Subjects: LCSH: Medical care—United States. | Health services
    administration—United States.
Classification: LCC RA395.A3 L4145 2023 (print) | LCC RA395.A3 (ebook) |
    DDC 362.10973—dc23/eng/20221114
LC record available at https://lccn.loc.gov/2022033878
LC ebook record available at https://lccn.loc.gov/2022033879

McGraw Hill books are available at special quantity discounts to use as premiums and sales promotions or for use in corporate training programs. To contact a representative, please visit the Contact Us pages at www.mhprofessional.com.

McGraw Hill is committed to making our products accessible to all learners. To learn more about the available support and accommodations we offer, please contact us at accessibility@mheducation.com. We also participate in the Access Text Network (www.accesstext.org), and ATN members may submit requests through ATN.

To the memory of my parents,
Thomas H. Lee and Kin Ping Lee,
immigrants who understood the meaning of
excellence and resilience

Contents

Preface

I'm a list maker by nature, so I'll lay out the context for this book by describing the top 10 reasons I love healthcare. I know healthcare has lots of problems, and the last few years have taken a terrible toll on the people working on its front lines. But there are good reasons why healthcare continues to attract such wonderful, hardworking, and kind people.

Here are my top 10:

1. **Patients really appreciate your work:** They come to you with problems and fears, and when you mitigate those problems and ease those fears, they know something good has happened. I don't really think patients should say, "Thank you for seeing me;" that is, after all, our job. But the fact is that medical issues have high stakes for patients, who tend to be grateful when we help them.

2. **Society respects us:** I think most people working in healthcare like it when they meet new people and are asked, "So, what do you do?" They tend to be proud to respond when

they are asked, "Where do you work?" For good reason, working in healthcare and its institutions is reliably a source of pride.

3. **The people are great:** It's fun to go to work and see people who combine lofty values with practical sensibilities. (We *do*, after all, have to deal with *everything* imaginable.) Burnout is a huge problem, but people in healthcare still routinely go way beyond their job descriptions to help patients and colleagues. They stay late. They lose sleep over patients' difficulties. They struggle to find solutions for terrible problems—and sometimes, they are able to solve problems.

4. **It keeps getting better:** There are so many diseases that were incurable early in my career that have become treatable, controllable, and even curable. The advance of science is thrilling. It adds complexity and costs to the work, but it's wonderful to be able to offer hope to patients who not so long ago would have faced a grim prognosis.

5. **The stakes are high:** The pressure to be perfect can be overwhelming at times, but the flip side of that coin is that the push for perfection brings a lot of pride. People in healthcare don't shy away from goals like zero harm. They know that no other goal is reasonable. They hate to make errors that harm patients, so much so that they are determined to acknowledge them and learn from them. I like that.

6. **You can be on a great team:** I'm not going to be on a legendary professional sports team or be a Navy SEAL. But it is still routinely possible for me and everyone else in healthcare to be part of a team that does a fantastic job

taking care of patients. Like great teams in other endeavors, the best healthcare teams have members who know each other, cover for each other, trust each other, and share pride in their accomplishments.

7. **You can feel the click when you get relationships right:** Sometimes a joke can deepen a relationship, but sometimes it can be a disaster. When you get to Chapter 6, you'll see an analysis of the use of humor at its best and worst. It shows the potentially wonderful impact of humor when there is a strong foundation of courtesy and respect in the clinician-patient relationship. You are always stepping across a line when you inject humor into an interaction, but patients who feel respected by their caregivers welcome you on the other side. Healthcare gives you the chance to get it right.

8. **You have the satisfaction of reducing suffering:** There is a lot of suffering in healthcare, and it goes beyond physical pain to include fear, anxiety, and confusion. When you work with patients, you have the chance every single day to reduce someone's suffering. This opportunity is there for doctors and nurses, of course, but also for all the people who interact with patients. That gives you something to feel good about as you commute home at the end of your day.

9. **You start from scratch with every single patient:** It has taken me years to appreciate that *real* satisfaction doesn't come from flashes of brilliance that might help an occasional patient. I am more impressed with my colleagues who rise to the occasion and give their best to every single patient. They remind me of great athletes who

bear down and focus on every single play, or musicians who do the equivalent. No matter what has happened in the past, the next patient gives you the chance to be the kind of caregiver you want to think of yourself as being.

10. **You have the chance to improve:** My late father told my brothers and me that the people he knew who were unhappy tended to feel like they were just hanging on. He said, "Don't ever let that happen to you." And he told us to find work where we could always feel that our trajectory was upward, that we were learning new things, and that we could be better next year than we are now. Healthcare offers that in spades.

Healthcare and society have been through a lot over the past few years, and there is likely plenty more turmoil ahead. But my hope is that these 10 reasons to love healthcare will remain intact. To that end, I've written this book focusing on key activities that I believe will be critical to preserving what is great about our work: building trust in patients and employees, broadening and deepening our concept of safety, and pursuing equity and inclusion to its logical and inspiring target (zero inequity). Society is changing around healthcare, and I also will discuss how we should respond to the evolution of consumers and our marketplaces.

The more things change, the more important it is that some things remain the same. I hope this book will help healthcare adapt to its challenges and remain the best type of work I can imagine.

Acknowledgments

IT IS NOT false humility when I note that my strength is not coming up with important ideas, but is instead recognizing them when others articulate them. With that dynamic in mind, I must start this section by acknowledging the enormous influence of my friends and colleagues who are working in their organizations to improve healthcare—making it better, more efficient, and more accessible.

These colleagues include people like the late Leon Haley, MD, the CEO of University of Florida Health in Jacksonville, whose comments about how preparations for a "100-day hurricane" at the beginning of the Covid-19 pandemic turned into something that lasted more than any of us could have imagined. I cannot list all the leaders, clinicians, and managers from healthcare delivery organizations whose work shapes this book. But I will mention how, on a visit to the emergency department of University of Rochester Medical Center in June 2022, I saw someone whose job is attending to the front entrance—helping people get out of cars, making sure they don't park in unloading zones, and so on. He was sweeping up the foyer inside the doors, and I learned that this wasn't actually part of his job; he did it all the time because he felt like it was his emergency department. Seeing acts like this and meeting people like him every day in healthcare constantly gives me a sense of what is possible in our challenging field.

These colleagues also include people I work with at Press Ganey, many of whose names come up frequently throughout this book. I work with a group of *thought leaders*—we cringe at this label—all forward-looking, all idealistic and optimistic, yet grounded in reality, often from having worked on the delivery side of healthcare for decades. I note many of their names throughout the book, but they all created or contributed enormously to the content. This group includes Mary Jo Assi, Michael Bennick, Rachel Biblow, Chrissy Daniels, Jeff Doucette, Jessica Dudley, Tejal Gandhi, Senem Guney, Deirdre Mylod, and Casey Willis-Abner as well as other colleagues whose work at Press Ganey touches on the experience of patients and the workforce, and issues like safety and equity.

As Press Ganey has evolved in recent years, it has added colleagues who are focused on consumerism and health insurers. They have been my teachers, and I can't list them all here. But I will just say that I have felt fortunate to be working at this company at this time, as the work we do immerses us in the gripping issues that fill this book. In fact, the suggestion to write something about how the work of reducing suffering had evolved in recent years came from my boss, Pat Ryan, the CEO of Press Ganey, and many of the key insights came from my colleagues Nell Buhlman and Darren Dworkin.

I also owe a lot to my colleagues at *NEJM Catalyst*, including Ed Prewitt, Namita Mohta, and Lisa Gordon. When I looked for examples of good work or important insights, I frequently found their work in this online spinoff from *The New England Journal of*

Medicine, which we created to accelerate progress toward a higher-value healthcare system. The clarity of the writing and power of the ideas is due to their work.

As with my other recent books, I enjoyed working with Beverly Merz, who edits and prepares my manuscripts, and Casey Ebro at McGraw Hill. Social network analysis has demonstrated that Broadway plays are more likely to succeed when the key actors, producers, and director have worked together before. I think the same dynamic is apparent with my collaboration with Bev and Casey.

Introduction

I'LL START BY listing six themes upon which I hope this book will provide useful insights, and then I will turn to why I think it is potentially valuable to step back and consider them. The six themes that are going to come up over and over in this book are:

1. Excellence

2. Trust

3. Respect

4. Inclusion

5. Resilience

6. Reliability

I'll confess that I've tossed these words around pretty casually throughout my career, and even taken them for granted. For example, I knew my colleagues and I were good people who were working hard, so I assumed that people would trust us.

But the events of the last few years—the Covid-19 pandemic, the murder of George Floyd, climate disasters, and more—have shown that nothing can be taken for granted anymore. If organizations and individuals are to maintain a high quality of care during times of uncertainty, they must rethink what these words mean. And they must work to make them organizational norms.

Healthcare has entered a new phase in terms of quality assessment. In the past, quality was routinely regarded as unmeasurable, and best achieved by recruiting good people, supporting them in their work, and protecting their autonomy. Then, around the turn of this century, two landmark reports from the Institute of Medicine— *To Err Is Human*[1] and *Crossing the Quality Chasm*[2]—exposed US healthcare as being far from ideal and showed that there was much to be done to improve the safety and quality of care.[3] That introduced a second phase, in which healthcare leaders began to explore performance management and the principles of high reliability.

That work is far from complete, but a third phase has been ushered in by challenges that became apparent in early 2020. In truth, the Covid-19 pandemic was not a bifurcating event. By the start of the pandemic, burnout in the healthcare workforce was already a tremendous concern, and inequity in healthcare was a source of anger long before millions watched George Floyd die on the streets of Minneapolis.

But there is a new intensity to these issues now. They have become operational imperatives for organizations invested in the excellence of their care. Many healthcare organizations have come to view staffing issues—which are intertwined with concerns about safety, equity, and inclusion—as existential threats. Those issues are not really new, but now they are severe enough to threaten institutions' abilities to staff beds and answer phones, and the nuances of their implications have come into sharper focus.

The last few years have also shown that healthcare just isn't as reliable as it must be. Even in the best circumstances, it isn't easy to deliver care that is reliably safe, effective, efficient, and empathic. Doing so when delivery models must be redesigned on the fly takes *real* organizational resilience. It means going beyond being an HRO (high-reliability organization) to becoming an HRO-NMW (high-reliability organization, no matter what).

How to become an HRO-NMW? Two essential initial steps are:

1. **Clarify the organization's strategic goal:** What is it trying to do and for whom? In healthcare, the overarching goal is reducing patients' suffering, alleviating not just physical pain but also fear, confusion, and anxiety. Achieving that goal requires making every effort to extend life and improve health. When doing so is impossible, it means giving people the assurance that things are as good as they could be, given the cards that they have been dealt.

2. **Define the value chain of activities:** These activities include ensuring the technical excellence of care, of course, and they also include building trust. Even when care is technically excellent, patients suffer when they do not trust that their care will be safe, and that all their caregivers will understand their concerns, respect them, and work together to meet their needs.

Reliably earning patients' trust is impossible unless providers have also earned the trust of caregivers (i.e., their employees, affiliated clinicians, and other personnel). And *that* work requires broader and deeper efforts to improve safety and equity, and demonstrating a commitment to these values, no matter what.

Our work is cut out for us. We have much to learn and much to do to earn the trust of patients and employees during the era that lies ahead. This book seeks to provide a road map for the process of learning and improvement.

I paused when writing that last sentence, wondering whether I should use the word *transformation* instead of *improvement*. I eschewed *transformation* because I know how that word plays with exhausted caregivers just trying to get through their week's responsibilities. I also know that many experienced clinicians have been told throughout their careers that transformation was underway, and when they look up a few years later, things seem pretty much the same.

That said, this moment may be different, and *transformation* may be what the times call for and what is upon us. Two big-picture observations combine to support this suspicion. The first is the observation that "every system is perfectly designed to get the results it gets."[4] That observation emphasizes the need to develop systemic changes to produce systemic improvements. (You don't get better results by creating incentives or pressuring people to work harder.)

The other is the work of the late John Nash, whose extraordinary story was the focus of the book and movie *A Beautiful Mind*. Nash won the Nobel Prize for Economics in 1994 for describing an equilibrium concept for noncooperative games in which binding agreements cannot be written. In a Nash equilibrium, multiple parties are frozen in current relationships because no party can change its strategies while the other parties keep their strategies unchanged. Nash equilibriums break down when the pain of the status quo for multiple parties exceeds their fear of the unknown.

Nash's concept suggests that now is the moment when systemic change will come to healthcare because so many parties find the status quo to be painful, and, in many organizations, something approaching transformation seems to be underway. The pressures for change became implicit in media accounts of healthcare's response during Covid-19 surges: facilities that were understaffed and overwhelmed, healthcare professionals who were working through exhaustion, patients who endured hours or even days in the ER because there were not enough staff to see them or enough available rooms to admit them, people in crisis waiting weeks for beds in mental health facilities, which were understaffed and overwhelmed, too.

Surges and other crises come and go, but recently they seemed to just keep coming and coming. No one knows what will happen next, but we do know that healthcare organizations must structure themselves to do more than function smoothly during periods of calm. Real excellence requires resilience and the ability to adapt. Organizations need to assess how well prepared they are for crisis—and then work to become even better prepared.

As someone who trained in cardiology, I see the last few years as the equivalent of a stress test for healthcare organizations. No one actually passes or fails a cardiac stress test; the treadmill goes faster and faster, and the incline is increased until the patient cannot continue. Everyone eventually hits their wall. The question is how far can they go, and what makes them stop. Is it their heart? Is it their lungs? Is it pain in their knees? The results guide patients and their doctors on what health issues to address and how to become healthier.

Similarly, the stresses of the last few years have unmasked previously unrecognized areas for improvement in every organization. Some organizations are doing better than others, and data show a "separation of the pack" on important metrics. For example, the gap between the median and the 90th percentile for physician alignment with their organization nearly doubled between 2018 and 2021. (More on that in Chapter 7.) But we're learning lessons that can help every organization look forward and prepare for change.

There are some signs that the early years of this decade have produced changes so profound that the old ways of conducting business are never coming back:

- **Influx of electronic messages:** The volume of electronic messages from patients to their physicians rose about 150 percent in the first weeks after the Covid-19 pandemic began and has remained at that level.[5] In fact, patient messaging was slowly building over the last decade, and was increasingly identified as a cause of physician burnout. But during the pandemic-imposed isolation, patients of all ages figured out how to use patient portals and how to reach their healthcare providers in other ways as well. These patients have a lot of questions, and healthcare organizations are still scrambling to figure out how to meet their information needs.

- **Reliance on the internet:** Patients got used to using the internet 24/7 for things other than reaching their clinicians. They are now functioning as consumers, people who have choices. They are *researching* their physicians and hospitals and gathering information on their tests and treatments. They have become much more sophisticated. (Consider how widespread public understanding of the differences among PCR, antigen, and antibody testing is today.) The era in which discussions of knotty medical issues ending with the advice to "ask your doctor" is about to end. Today, episodes of care often begin when patients start a search on Google.

- **Acceptance of telemedicine:** Telemedicine visits shot up at the beginning of the Covid-19 pandemic, subsequently decreased, and have plateaued at 10 to 15 percent of visits. Press Ganey data have shown from the start that patients give high ratings to their clinicians during telemedicine visits, but they give lower ratings to telemedicine's logistics (e.g., the ease of logging on). After about a year, data show that patients and providers are getting better at using telemedicine at many—but not all—institutions. Clearly, some organizations are working at improving how telemedicine functions for clinicians and patients, and others are not.

- **Employee churn:** Workforce turnover in the entire country reached amazing levels in late 2021. Four and a half million Americans quit their jobs in November 2021—a record high. These data are actually evidence of the robustness of the economy; people often leave their jobs because they find better opportunities elsewhere. That is good news for workers, but it poses obvious challenges for healthcare organizations trying to find the personnel to staff their floors and offices.

- **Increasing concern for diversity, equity, and inclusion (DEI):** The murder of George Floyd in May 2020 led to a long-overdue surge of concern about the centuries-old problem of DEI. Appropriately, that concern continues to build, and understanding of its importance is deepening. Press Ganey recently published data showing that employee perceptions of an organization's inclusiveness are strongly related to their likelihood of staying there. That powerful trend cut across every job type. The data were similar for physicians and for security personnel.

Around the country, organizations are recognizing the constant change in their environments, and redesigning the ways in which they make plans, manage, and work. Some telling signs of redesign are:

- **Hardwiring nimbleness:** Many organizations now realize that they can't make big decisions only at annual budget time. Several have moved to quarterly goal setting, and modified budget management to allow quarterly adjustments.

- **Planning for change:** When change is perpetual, a structure is always going to be designed for last year's challenges. Healthcare organizations will *always* need to bring in new employees—and retrain current employees—for new roles. This is one reason Mayo Clinic has made acquiring the ability to "transform" one of its three main strategic goals for the decade ahead.[6]

- **Restructuring care redesign accountability:** Healthcare leaders have realized that they must not only be nimble, but they must also be effective in implementing care redesigns. As one chief medical officer put it, "Once we realized that Covid-19 was not just going to last a few months, but was probably going to go on for years, we understood that we couldn't have 32 different hospitals figuring out on their own how to redesign orthopedic care. And we couldn't have medical directors who might only know a little about orthopedics telling orthopedists what they needed to do. We needed to move to an orthopedic service line that really meant something and do the same for other major areas."

- **Shaping workforce wellness and culture:** To recruit and retain excellent employees, organizations have been taking a wide array of steps, from rethinking roles (especially in nursing); to making real progress on achieving DEI; to building teams; to developing special programs for some segments (e.g., support for women physicians). These steps are all good steps. There is no magic bullet to address all workforce challenges.

- **Moving toward value-based contracting and care delivery:** The first few years of this decade have seen an acceleration of the movement away from fee-for-service payment toward contracting agreements that reward quality and efficiency. As a result, provider organizations are ramping up their population-management programs and creating the infrastructure to manage care.

- **Developing a data strategy appropriate for the challenges:** To become nimble and more effective, organizations need data. For example, in the past, many organizations measured workforce engagement once a year—or even less often. And some organizations were reluctant to measure it at all during the stressful early months of the Covid-19 pandemic. Once organizations realized that the pandemic and related stress were not ending, they began to survey subsets of the workforce more frequently to guide interventions.[7]

As healthcare organizations adjust to change, the word that keeps coming up is *trust*. Leaders know that their success will not be solely determined by their volume of office visits or hospitalizations, even though the payment system may still emphasize those metrics. Organizations can succeed only if they retain or increase their market share, which both require patient loyalty. In times of turmoil, earning that loyalty requires winning and retaining patients' trust.

Trust is something that people working in healthcare used to take for granted because they know they are good people who are working hard. That might have been enough in calmer times, but when so many things are changing, trust is tested. Patients have to wonder when care is redesigned on the fly whether they will really receive the attention they need.

How do organizations build trust in an era in which staffing is short, the wait for appointments is long, and care models are constantly changing? Patients must wonder if their needs might get lost in the shuffle—and the fact is that *no one* in healthcare should ever wonder if their needs have been forgotten or are being ignored.

In this book I'll describe the transformations underway and how healthcare organizations are responding. I'll use data to demonstrate trends and offer insights on interventions likely to drive improvement, provide examples of organizations making major advances, and make recommendations for how healthcare leaders, clinicians, and other personnel can use these findings to shape their path forward.

In Part I of this book, I will focus on what has happened during the first three years of this decade, including the pressures produced by the intertwined storms described above, and how healthcare has responded. In Part II I will look forward and describe the remodeling that I believe healthcare organizations must do in the decade ahead. And in Part III, I'll detail specific ways in which healthcare organizations can create value for patients and their workforces, such as building trust, improving safety, and advancing the equity and inclusiveness of their cultures.

HEALTHCARE'S
PATH FORWARD

PART I

THE RECENT PAST (2020–2022)

CHAPTER 1

Crisis upon Crisis

IN EARLY MARCH 2020, Leon Haley told me how his health system was preparing for Covid-19. Haley was the CEO of University of Florida Health in Jacksonville, Florida, an emergency medicine physician by training, and one of my favorite people in healthcare—smart, honest, and confident, yet humble. Covid-19 had not yet arrived in Florida in force; the first surge in Jacksonville would come in early July 2020. But he was worried—very worried—and he used the strongest metaphor he could think of to describe his team's frame of mind.

"We're getting ready for something like a 100-day hurricane," he said.

One year later, we recalled that conversation in a podcast interview, and reflected on how we had underestimated Covid-19 and other challenges of 2020. He described how much he had learned from sustaining a crisis response over a period that was already more than a year. He still thought the hurricane metaphor was appropriate, but only partially so.[1]

"In Florida, one of the things you have to learn is how to manage during a hurricane," he said. "There's physical damage. And then there's the economic toll. Finally, there's the piece that impacts your staff, where some of our staff can't get to work, or they have trouble at home, or they lose their homes.

"But, typically, you are in and then you are out with a hurricane," he said. "With Covid-19, in the first couple of months we were getting more and more patients. Then the state put a lockdown on elective surgeries and procedures, and that created a financial hit.

"And then it exploded," he said. "I can remember it vividly," he continued. "We got to mid-June, and we had just six patients. But on July 4th weekend, we went from 25 patients on Friday to 45 on Saturday to 65 on Sunday. By Monday, we were in the 80s, on our way to 113 in mid-July.

"Suddenly, in July and August, we had a lot more deaths. Patients were a lot sicker, requiring a lot more intensive therapy. It took a toll on our staff. We had nurses who realized that they were old enough for retirement, and they chose to retire. We had people step away from healthcare."

By all accounts, Haley was an extraordinary leader for his organization through the "hurricane" as the 100 days turned to 300. He learned how to communicate throughout a sustained crisis, avoiding information overload yet delivering key messages at critical moments. On December 14, 2020, he became the first person in Florida to be vaccinated against Covid-19. The event was televised, which helped him to send a signal to other Black Americans that the vaccine was safe.

On July 25, 2021, Haley died in an accident while taking a rare day off—some say it was his *first* day off since the pandemic began. He was just 56 years old.

On UF Health Jacksonville's Facebook page, staff members were invited to leave thoughts and memories. One ICU nurse described how Haley had "spent his last day at the hospital walking unit to unit, administering the Covid-19 vaccine himself in an effort to protect his staff." Another staffer wrote that Haley's death was an "unimaginable loss," adding, "I have never felt as inspired to be a leader and being a leader as I have since he has been our CEO and Dean."

Haley's leadership evolved right up until the end, and he was quite aware of changes to his approach. "I've learned to step back and ask, 'If I were coming into this new, what would I do differently?'" he said in our last interview. "I've only been here four years, but that's just long enough to get into a pattern. I have had to think how I would do things if I were coming into this brand new."

As was true for Haley, the crises of the last few years have caused many in healthcare to rethink the nature of their work. In doing so, they have been forced to confront challenges not only related to Covid-19 and the resulting supply chain disruption, but also presented by an array of destabilizing trends in other areas including:

- **Social unrest:** calls to improve diversity, equity, and inclusiveness in delivering care and in the healthcare workplace, and a growing distrust of science

- **Political divisiveness:** the polarization of the electorate and legislative gridlock

- **Consumerism:** patients' increasing use of the internet to gather information that guides choices and shapes their expectations around care

- **Demographic shifts:** the aging of baby boomers with the concomitant increase in demands for excellence in chronic disease care

- **Workforce drain:** staffing difficulties resulting from a decrease in loyalty to employers

- **Environmental disasters:** the health consequences of climate change and acute weather events

The short-term challenges are daunting, consuming, and at times overwhelming. Patients are filling emergency departments and intensive care units. Doctors, nurses, and other frontline caregivers are burned out, frightened, and in short supply. Employees of all types are leaving their jobs, sometimes because better ones have become available, and sometimes because they just don't feel like staying in their roles.

The result can be a management nightmare. Patients cannot leave the emergency department because there are no empty beds in the rest of the hospital; they cannot be discharged because there are no personnel to care for them at their homes or in skilled nursing facilities. Employees and patients are anxious about when they can get the next dose of Covid-19 vaccines, or, conversely, they are upset about requirements to get vaccinated. Costs of personal protective equipment (PPE), testing, vaccinations, and other healthcare necessities are rising, but revenue is uncertain.

These are the "hurricane issues," the challenges that healthcare leaders and managers must hunker down and work through to the best of their abilities. They can draw some comfort from knowing that storms always end, and there will be some way through every crisis. Nothing can go on forever.

But for healthcare organizations to emerge in good shape on the other side of any given crisis, they must address the broad, long-term issues that redefine the nature of excellence itself. The trust that had once been taken for granted is eroding. Organizations must respond to changes in how people use the internet to meet their needs. And they must adapt to fundamental changes in the healthcare marketplace that have accelerated because of the disruption of these times.

In this chapter I'll describe some major themes that have arisen via recent challenges—themes that must be part of healthcare organizations' efforts to pursue excellence in the era ahead.

Trust

The erosion of trust in virtually all institutions, which has been a major worldwide trend since the 1970s, has accelerated enormously during the past several years, and has affected even healthcare and science. Over the last decade, political leaders have talked relentlessly about "fake news," and cable news programs have presented starkly different versions of the same events. Still, it was a shock for many in healthcare when so many patients—and about 30 percent of their own workforces—were hesitant to get vaccinated for Covid-19. They did not trust scientists, physicians, and their leaders who maintained that the vaccines' benefits far outweighed the risks, and that widespread use was important for curbing the pandemic.

Vaccine hesitancy due to the erosion of trust in healthcare is a reflection of worrisome social trends. As journalist Matthew Yglesias noted in a January 2022 article with the memorable title "All Kinds of Bad Behavior Is on the Rise," there are ongoing epidemics of dangerous driving, disruptive behavior in schools, and attacks on flight attendants and restaurant workers.[2]

The article notes that attacks on healthcare workers have also increased—an observation supported by reports from around the country. For example, the CEO of one New England delivery system told me in the summer of 2021 that 10 nurses had resigned from its flagship hospital in the past two months because they were assaulted or groped by patients or patients' family members.

In these times, trust is tested and it matters more than ever. Patients cannot have peace of mind without trusting their caregivers. And caregivers cannot inspire trust unless they trust their colleagues, leaders, and organizations. Clinicians and others in healthcare must recognize how critical trust is to our work and think seriously about how to earn and build it. We can no longer assume that we will be trusted because of who we are and our track records.

So what *is* trust, and what do we know about building it? Trust is sometimes described as confidence that a person will be treated fairly, even in situations that we can't imagine. Trust depends on more than perfect performance under ideal circumstances; it requires being highly reliable even when circumstances are extraordinary. That type of high reliability requires a culture that refuses to surrender its values when problems arise, that learns from setbacks, and that is ready to innovate and adapt.

For patients, trust means they can be confident that their caregivers will do their best to keep them safe and meet their needs, no matter what. For people working in healthcare, trust in their organizations means they can be confident that they will be safe and supported when delivering the best possible care, no matter what.

By its very nature, building trust in healthcare is a group activity. Clinicians must be able to rely on each other and on nonclinical staff to support operations. Operational processes must be in place to ensure consistency. Managers must ensure that the system operates efficiently.

To be honest, even before Covid-19, workforce trust was declining. Data collected by Press Ganey engagement surveys showed marked variability in how workers felt about their organizations' commitment to quality, safety, and teamwork. Moreover, within organizations, there was marked variability depending on job type, race, ethnicity, and gender, and leaders took notice because they realized that workforce engagement was a critical determinant of all types of performance. Then, during the first frightening months of the Covid-19 pandemic, several types of experiences influenced trust in the workforce—positively and negatively.

On the positive side, frontline clinicians watched each other rise to the occasion and figure out how to meet patients' needs in extreme circumstances. At the hospital where I work, nurses brought shopping bags of baby monitors into the ICUs during the first days of the first surge so they could hear patients behind closed doors, and thus consume less precious PPE going in and out of rooms. When you see colleagues using their creativity like that to solve problems for patients, you trust them, and you want them to trust you.

Many organizations anticipated the fears and the adverse effects that the pandemic would have on their employees, and they took steps both to show their concern and mitigate harm. For example, many organizations made commitments that there would be no layoffs; others developed childcare and mental health support initiatives to help address stresses on their personnel.

However, for myriad reasons, some organizations lost their employees' trust. For example, they didn't provide sufficient PPE or testing supplies, imposed overwhelming workloads, placed inexperienced staff in difficult situations, and failed to provide job security. Staff discontent was amplified by social media. Faced with such pressures, many organizations began looking for a framework that they could use to earn and build trust.

One simple and practical model for trust was published in May 2020, in the first months of the Covid-19 pandemic and around the same time as the murder of George Floyd.[3] It was authored by Harvard Business School professor Frances Frei, who also delivered a widely viewed TED talk closely related to the framework in her paper.[4]

Frei's framework describes three key drivers of trust: authenticity, logic, and empathy. Organizational research shows that workforces are more trusting when they understand their organization's motivations and believe they are authentic. For this reason, healthcare leaders must have clear ideas of their most important values and convey those values in all they do. This authenticity must then be supplemented by proof that leaders care about their colleagues (empathy) and have a rational and informed basis for their actions (logic).

Applying this framework from the perspective of patients would suggest that they want their caregivers to grasp their fears and what they are going through, and to prove with their actions that their concerns are authentic. And then, patients hope, the caregivers will show that they are effective in meeting patients' needs.

From the perspective of healthcare employees, the hope is that their organizations grasp and really do care about *their* fears and needs (e.g., the problem of finding childcare when sitters have Covid-19) and are effective in coming up with solutions.

Building trust among employees is not the single answer to challenges that healthcare organizations have in recruiting and retaining nurses and other employees, but the data described below make clear that it is an important part of a multidimensional approach to workforce issues. Most striking in those analyses is that the issues that seemed the highest priority in determining employees' likelihood of staying at an organization are closely related to those that create trust, while compensation ranked near the bottom.

Safety

Concerns about safety in hospital care became a high priority at many healthcare organizations with the IOM reports at the turn of the century, which illuminated systematic safety breaches in hospitals. But the Covid-19 pandemic ushered in a new phase in which concerns about safety have evolved, intensified, and extended to new arenas. These changes reflect patients' and caregivers' fears about their risk of being infected as well as uncertainty with new care delivery models.

Experienced healthcare managers who might have thought they had already seen everything faced new issues as the spread of Covid-19 became difficult to contain. Almost immediately, hospitals shut down visitation to minimize the spread of infection. This step made perfect sense, but the unintended consequences were hard to imagine in advance.

For example, on consecutive nights in the first few weeks of the pandemic, I had two elderly men who were my primary care patients admitted to Boston hospitals with strokes. Their wives brought them to the emergency departments, but then could not stay with them. The separations created anguish for all four of them that I will not soon forget. But banning hospital visitors also led to an increase in falls and other safety events in hospitals around the country. Clinicians suddenly realized how much "work" family members did to support care while keeping patients company.

The intensification of safety concerns reflected the fear generated by a new disease that was poorly understood and, initially, seemingly unpreventable and untreatable. In 2019, a bathroom in a hospital that was less than perfectly clean might have been seen as unpleasant. In 2020, it was nothing less than frightening. Seeing litter in a hallway or a fluid stain on a clinician's scrubs, patients could not help but wonder whether they were they safe.

The extension of safety concerns meant that safety was no longer just an issue for hospital care—it also was a concern in ambulatory settings and with new care delivery models such as telemedicine. In the past, we took safety in the ambulatory setting for granted because it seemed that the stakes were so much higher in the inpatient setting. After all, hospitalized patients were more fragile and experiencing more tests, treatments, diagnostics, and other types of care. In fact, there was so little concern about outpatient safety that the standard patient experience surveys for medical practices endorsed by the US CAHPS didn't include a single question about safety.

Nevertheless, some experts had argued for decades that ambulatory safety was important. Among the most prominent was Tejal Gandhi, MD, my colleague at Press Ganey. She had been making this point as an academic researcher and then as the leader of the National Patient Safety Foundation and at the Institute for Healthcare Improvement (IHI).[5] But interest in ambulatory safety remained lukewarm at best.

Now, her moment had arrived.

During the pandemic, Press Ganey offered clients the option to add to surveys questions that captured whether patients were unnerved by safety issues during ambulatory visits. Examples of these survey items (for which patients were asked to express their level of agreement on a 1–5 scale) included:

- The staff addressed your concerns for your safety at the facility during the Covid-19 crisis.

- You are confident that staff provided care in a safe and secure manner.

- Staff cleaned (using gel or soap/water) their hands before caring for you.

The magnitude of the importance of safety concerns on patient loyalty has been startling. In our analyzes of more than 12 million surveys performed after outpatient visits, 83.3 percent of patients had no safety concerns, and their overall provider rankings were often in the 99th percentile. But for the 16.7 percent of patients who had *any* safety concerns at all, the likelihood of recommending the provider was as low as the first percentile.

When the analysis was repeated on the subset of more than nine million patients who gave their physicians perfect ratings for their work, safety concerns were reported by 6.7 percent of patients. Although patients in this group considered the physician care top notch, their likelihood of recommending the provider was only in the second percentile.

The data are striking, but the comments from patients related to safety bring their hopes and fears to life. Here is an example of a positive comment: "I am very impressed with the precautions taken for cleaning and disinfecting the waiting area and the exam room was spotless." Before Covid-19, I can't recall seeing comments like this about ambulatory care.

I also had never seen negative comments like this one: "There was no social distance seating. There was no wiping of waiting room or anyplace else." Or this one: "The room I was escorted to was not cleaned up from prior patients. I should not be placed in a room where the table for the patient is still dirty, with used syringe and medication and alcohol wipes still on the counter."

And it wasn't just patient feedback. Press Ganey data from surveys of the workforce showed that caregivers valued the same things as patients, and were unnerved by the same things, too.

Equity

Racism and other forms of bias have been sources of injustice in American society and elsewhere for centuries or more, but the murder of George Floyd demonstrated how video captured on smartphones helps people grasp horror and feel empathy. The ensuing discussions and data analyses produced insights that startled even people in healthcare who considered themselves progressive on social issues.

The painful key insights for healthcare leaders include:

- **Being "color blind" is not enough:** Even if individuals and organizations treat everyone the same, that does not undo the effects of racism and other types of bias. Ibram X. Kendi's book *How to Be an Antiracist* became popular reading in healthcare organizations, and I suspect that many of my colleagues bought the book hoping that it would be an efficient way to affirm that they were not doing anything wrong. Instead, it lays out an ambitious lifelong agenda aimed at undoing the policies that drive racism.

- **We are not color blind, even when we think we are:** Data collected by Press Ganey, client organizations, and healthcare researchers paint unsettling pictures. For example, it seems overwhelmingly clear that pain is not taken as seriously by caregivers when reported by patients who are members of underrepresented groups as when reported by whites. Survey data demonstrate that non-white patients report worse pain control than white patients do, but other data show that they receive lower amounts of opioids. The CEO of a leading urban safety-net hospital recently said to me, "We were shocked when we looked at our own data. I mean, giving good care to these populations is at the core of how we see ourselves."

- **Diversity, equity, and inclusion (DEI) is not just about race, and it's not just about patients:** Press Ganey data collected from employees show that ratings of organizations' DEI culture are lower for women than for men, lower for every other racial/ethnic group than for whites, and lower for every job type than for managers. Even among employees who self-identified as Black or another racial ethnic group, the managers were more likely to have a rosy view of the DEI culture of the organization than were personnel in other roles.

- **The senior management teams of healthcare organizations look like the C-suites in other sectors— predominantly white and predominantly male:**[6] These senior management teams do not look demographically like the patients they serve, and they don't look like the current healthcare workforce or the one in the pipelines either. For example, the percentage of current hospital leaders who are white is 88 percent, versus 49 percent of medical school enrollees. And the percentages who are male are 65 percent and 48 percent, respectively.

- **Diversity is a performance issue:** "Lack of diversity makes you stupid," one CEO recently told me, adding, "I hate being stupid." He was alluding to the insight that everyone has blind spots, and that if you have a diverse team, and everyone's voice is heard, your collective blind spots should be reduced. That insight is supported by management data showing that more diverse management teams are associated with better organizational performance.

- **DEI is a workforce retention issue:** Press Ganey data from a survey of 410,000 employees in 2021 showed that how employees rated the DEI of their organizational culture correlated strongly with their intent to stay. DEI ratings also correlated strongly with overall engagement and safety culture. These correlations were evident across all job types (physicians and security personnel had essentially the same statistical profile). Overall, employees that gave low ratings to the organization on DEI were 4.6 times as likely to indicate that they were likely to leave. High on the list of predictors of who might leave were low scores on statements like "My work is meaningful," "This organization provides high-quality care and service," and "This organization treats employees with respect." Surprisingly weak predictors were low rankings on questions about adequate staffing and competitive salaries.

It is more important than ever to staff units adequately and to pay salaries that are competitive and fair. Those are the bare minimum of what it takes to get employees in the door. But to keep them from leaving, consider how much they value the items in the list above and the diversity, equity, and inclusion of the organizational culture.

Consumerism

Ask any doctor how they knew that Covid-19 was transforming the way in which their patients interact with healthcare, and they will likely bring up the frequency with which their patients send them messages or ask questions electronically. Data from EPIC users across the country showed that messages via patient portals went up 150 percent almost immediately when Covid-19 hit, and they have stayed up.[7] Patients of all ages had to meet their needs without leaving home—and once they realized that Amazon would deliver many things in a day or two, and that they could get information from their doctors without in-person visits, there was no going back.

Offices were not prepared for the flood of messages, and many are still adjusting. But the uptick in messaging is just one manifestation of the public's growing comfort with and reliance on the internet. A September 2021 Press Ganey survey found the following:

- **Digital drives choice:** Patients rely on digital resources 2.2 times more than provider referrals when choosing a healthcare provider.

- **Ratings matter:** 84 percent of respondents said they would not see a referred provider who had less than a four-star rating.

- **Patients are growing comfortable with virtual health:** More than one-third of patients had used telehealth in the past year—a 338 percent increase since 2019.

- **Patients see themselves as customers:** Assuming quality of care is perceived as good, 70.8 percent of patients rate customer service and 63 percent rate communication as more important than bedside manner when it comes to a defining a five-star experience.

- **Shopping for healthcare:** On average, consumers use three different websites during healthcare research and read 5.5 reviews before making a decision.

One of my physician colleagues recently asked, "What *is* the difference between a consumer and a patient? Aren't my patients still my patients?"

My response: Yes, they are still your patients. But *consumers* behave as if they have *choices*, while a lot of the time we assume that patients are going to do what we recommend. And I showed him this email from one of my patients—I'll call her Mary—whom I had recently referred to a neurosurgeon, gastroenterologist, and ENT physician for an array of issues:

Dear Dr. Lee:

I really appreciate the referrals you provided me. I left a message for [GI physician] and for [ENT physician]. I researched Dr. [neurosurgeon]. There is a consistency in his many negative reviews: "Rushed . . . Kept looking at his Apple Watch and phone . . . Didn't review history," etc. Normally I ignore negative ratings unless there is the same theme in all of them.

I have my eye on two neurosurgeons. I have calls in to both of them. I have a feeling that it's going to be a challenge to secure an appointment without the proper introduction and I believe time is of the essence due to the proximity of the bone to my spine and the fact that it has gotten worse.

Again, thank you so much for all your support and help.

Best regards,

Mary

In essence, she had taken my recommendations into account, and gone with most of them. For the neurosurgeon, she had done her own research and wanted my help getting in the door. I gave it to her. My colleague who asked about consumers and patients was still a bit hazy about the distinction between the two but agreed that my patient, acting as a consumer, had done the right thing, and said he would do the same.

Market Changes

Covid-19 and equity concerns have accelerated the shift of the US healthcare marketplace away from fee-for-service payment. Political leaders decided early on that no one should be deprived of testing, vaccination, or treatment for Covid-19 because of financial issues. Yet the downturn in the economy did not produce an increase in the proportion of uninsured Americans as might have been expected. Data through the spring of 2021 show that the uninsured rate in the United States remained steady at 11 percent through the early years of the pandemic.[8]

However, the form of insurance is changing. More people have public insurance (Medicare or Medicaid), while the proportion who have employer-based insurance has been declining. The percentage of Americans on Medicare who are covered by Medicare Advantage plans rose 9 percent from 2021 to 2022 and is shortly expected to exceed 50 percent, and there is a rapid transition in many states toward Managed Medicaid plans.[9]

The net effect of the shift from commercial insurance toward managed government insurance plans is marketplace pressure on healthcare providers to organize themselves so that they can work in contracts that have some basis other than fee-for-service. The advantage of fee-for-service is that it is relatively straightforward to implement. The disadvantage is that it is hard to adapt that model to improving quality or anything else, because the focus is upon money and the volume of services. The shutdown of in-person care during the Covid-19 pandemic showed providers that fee-for-service puts them at enormous financial risk when external circumstances make business as usual impossible. As one organization's leader put it, "We realized that we need a diversified portfolio of how we get paid so we can weather storms like Covid-19."

There are many models in use, but nearly all demand deeper cooperation—and even complete integration—between payers and providers. One problem is that, even when payers and providers have the best of intentions, it is hard to meet patients' needs efficiently. In the past, both payers and providers have been frustrated by the sense that barriers to improvement lay just outside their spans of control. Payers complained that providers didn't give their members timely access to care. Providers complained that payers' policies on what they would cover tortured them and their patients.

During the Covid-19 pandemic, however, virtually every stakeholder in healthcare stepped up and focused on meeting the needs of patients, and was ready to collaborate with other organizations, including competitors or natural adversaries. For example, not many patients or providers have asked how testing and vaccination came to be offered free, but insurance companies working with state and federal governments made them possible almost without anyone noticing.

This positive experience with cooperation bodes well for the ability of healthcare stakeholders to work together across the value chain of activities that are necessary to meet patients' needs. In this context, managing interdependencies becomes as important as managing within the walls of an organization. That dynamic is likely to be true in healthcare well into the future.

To make such collaborations occur more naturally, there is a movement underway toward payer and provider integration. Some of these organizations are provider organizations, like Geisinger Health System, that have developed an insurance arm (Geisinger Health Plan). Others are insurance companies that now employ large physician groups, like United Health's Optum Care Network. But even when payers and providers are not formally integrated, there is still a movement toward collaborating in ways that create value for patients as if they *were* integrated. And even when payers and providers *are* integrated, they virtually always know there is much more that they can do to improve the ways in which they work together.

One of the highest-priority metrics that they are focusing on together is member/patient experience, which is important both for health plans and for healthcare provider organizations.

But beyond its impact on growth, member experience is a major determinant of funding for insurance programs such as Medicare Advantage. When data are used to identify the factors that are crucial in improving the experience of health plan members, most of those identified are either directly or largely under the influence of healthcare providers. (See Chapter 11 for a deeper discussion of this topic.)

In summary, because of the crises of the last few years, trust, safety, equity, consumerism, and market changes have created major challenges for healthcare's leaders. The next chapter describes their early responses.

CHAPTER 2

Healthcare's Immediate Responses

MANY PEOPLE IN healthcare can pinpoint the date when their lives were turned upside down by the Covid-19 pandemic. For me, it was March 12, 2020, when a talk I was supposed to give was canceled, the primary care center where I practice announced that all scheduled visits would be virtual, and the NCAA basketball tournament was called off.

I could tell something big was afoot.

In this chapter I describe the early responses of healthcare organizations to Covid-19, as they confronted challenges related to trust, safety, equity, consumerism, and the marketplace. During the first few months of the pandemic, we were operating without a playbook. Every organization's board and leadership team had to step back and assess what mattered most.

Naturally, their responses varied. In some organizations, top leaders immediately began walking the halls during every shift, thanking staff members in person and listening as employees described the stress and fear that the pandemic was creating in their lives. In other organizations, leaders were less visible; some even relocated with their families to vacation homes, appearing in Zoom meetings rather than in person.

Not surprisingly, early in the pandemic surveys designed to measure alignment—employee agreement with an organization's values and mission—and engagement—how invested employees are in helping to achieve the organization's goals—showed a separation of the pack. For example, when compared with similar data from prior years, surveys of 124,000 physicians in 2021 show that, overall, organizations' median score for physician alignment actually went *up* in 2021, despite the crushing pressures imposed by the pandemic. Physicians were exhausted, but they were proud to be in healthcare during a time of great need. The same pattern was apparent in engagement and alignment data when nurses and other types of employees—from clerical to maintenance to security— were surveyed. At the same time the gap between the median scores and the 90th or 10th percentiles nearly doubled. These trends suggest that, under stress, the best were getting better, and the worst were getting worse.

These findings reminded me of work by Professor Raffaella Sadun of Harvard Business School and her colleagues. In 2014, they published an article with the provocative title "Does Management Matter in Healthcare?"[1] That was a reasonable question in calmer times, when it seemed like many healthcare organizations were on cruise control, and the actions of senior leaders made only modest differences. But these data make clear that, as of 2020, the answer to Raffaella's question is "Yes—like never before."

Lessons Learned

At the 40th Annual J.P. Morgan Healthcare Conference, held virtually in 2022 for the second consecutive year, leaders from several major healthcare delivery systems described some of the major revelations from the first years of the decade. Michael Dowling, the CEO of Northwell Health, offered a list of lessons with implications for the future that, in more ordinary times, would have seemed dizzying in scope. For Dowling, the pandemic:

- Demonstrated the benefits of integrated systems of care

- Accelerated digital health as a priority

- Demonstrated the advantage of a culture of emergency preparedness

- Changed the nature of work locations

- Highlighted the problem of healthcare inequities

- Demonstrated the benefits of regulatory flexibility

- Promoted innovation and creativity

Similarly, Intermountain Healthcare's CEO, Marc Harrison, described how the pandemic had defined a series of strategic relationships, which he summarized as follows:

- Good health → good business

- Partnerships → acceleration

- Equitable outcomes → imperative

- Consumer experience → differentiator

- Scale and speed to action → strength

Presentations at the conference emphasized several common themes, including the importance of integrating healthcare systems around the goal of meeting patients' needs—as opposed to just bringing together provider organizations to amass market power for contract negotiations. The presentations also brought out the importance of rapid and effective decision-making, which is not always a characteristic of healthcare organizations.

The leaders at the J.P. Morgan Healthcare Conference recognized that the world had changed and would continue changing. The movement toward digital healthcare and the importance of the movement toward consumerism were common themes. Several of the leaders used language like "anytime, anywhere access," "immediate virtual response," "personalized service," and "self-service." And, more than in any prior year, there was a deep commitment to moving away from fee-for-service models and toward value-based payment models, including capitation.

The takeaway message was that major changes on multiple fronts are essential for the years ahead. Modest incremental improvements in current operations will not be sufficient to deliver the excellence demanded by patients, consumers, and the healthcare workforce. Already, as a result of these pressures, organizations have gone deeper in understanding the nature of trust, safety, consumerism, and the marketplace.

Earning Trust Among Patients

During the early phases of the Covid-19 pandemic, we gave extraordinary amounts of thought and attention to building trust among patients. When Covid-19 hit, clinicians immediately realized that patients would be deeply concerned about safety. They improvised and redesigned care to meet patients' needs while minimizing risks—quickly, creatively, effectively, and without concern about financial implications.

These redesigns of care reflected all three of Frances Frei's drivers of trust, beginning with empathy for patients' fears and needs. For example, when caregivers realized how upsetting it was for patients to be prevented from seeing their family members, they used iPads to set up video-based family visits. When caregivers grasped how frustrating it was for family members to be unable to ask questions of the patients' clinicians, caregivers organized family meetings via Zoom. These meetings allowed family members throughout the country to interact with the clinicians, the patient, and each other.[2] The meetings did more than meet patients' needs for communication; they also enabled coordination among caregivers and among families. As one of my patients said after such a meeting, "It is really nice to know that everyone is on the same page."

The redesigns of care delivery demonstrated the authenticity of caregivers' values. Frontline staff in the emergency departments and intensive care units were nothing less than heroic, and many paid a price in terms of their own health and well-being.

There were other instances of improvised care that no one could have anticipated before the pandemic. For example, osteoporosis specialists at Geisinger Health System didn't want to expose their frail elderly patients to risk of Covid-19 infection by having them come into the medical center for their twice-yearly injections of Prolia. At the same time, the clinicians didn't want their patients to miss their treatments. In the hospital parking lot, patients were tested and vaccinated for Covid-19 in drive-through tents, leading the osteoporosis specialists to ask, "Why can't our patients get Prolia injections that way?" Soon, patients could get drive-through Prolia injections in the hospital parking lot.

Another example of values in action occurred at medical centers where orthopedists found themselves idle because they couldn't perform elective operations. Rather than staying home to ride out the pandemic in safety with their families, many volunteered for proning teams, groups of medical staff that worked together to flip patients on ventilators onto their stomachs to improve blood oxygenation. It's not easy to turn over a critically ill patient who is connected to all sorts of lines and tubes, but orthopedists tend to be strong, which made them perfect additions to proning teams.

These types of efforts also reflected what Frei calls *logic*; patients could see that their caregivers' efforts made a difference. For example, providers were almost completely effective in preventing the spread of Covid-19 infection from one patient to another in healthcare settings. During the early days of the pandemic, when neither vaccines nor specific antiviral treatments for Covid-19 were available, caregivers were still able to support the most severely ill patients through their hospitalizations.

In her TED talk, Frei notes the importance of communication in building trust. For example, she notes, it is obviously important that leaders have a good plan that has a real shot at working. But, to build trust, they must also communicate their plan, so patients and employees believe that these leaders just might pull it off.

To spread hope, many cancer centers do something dramatic—like banging a gong that everyone can hear—when patients finish their courses of chemotherapy. In that same vein, leaders at Montefiore Medical Center in New York City decided to play music throughout the hospital every time they successfully discharged a Covid-19 patient during the early days of the pandemic when the challenges seemed overwhelming. "We wanted to let people know that things were not as bleak as they might have appeared, because we were actually having successes," said Andrew Racine, MD, the organization's chief medical officer.

Montefiore's leadership team had a brief conversation about what song they should play, and one of Racine's colleagues suggested Alicia Keys's "New York" from "Empire State of Mind." Soon, Montefiore workers were quoting lines from the song and tweeting about how many times it had been played on their shifts.

Soon after *that*, Keys noticed the tweets and replied on Twitter ("My heart flows wide open with the love I feel from this!!!!"). Then, Keys gave an open-air concert for the workforces of Montefiore and others fighting the pandemic in New York. (If you don't know this song, you might want to find it on YouTube and imagine hearing it while working through exhaustion during those very difficult days.)

The public response to such early efforts of healthcare workers was extraordinary. In many cities, people leaned out their windows at 7 p.m. every night, banging on pots to express their appreciation. In Press Ganey's data, there was an unprecedented surge in patients' ratings of their care, which have historically risen for most measures at a rate of about 1 percent per year. But in just one *month* (February 2020 to March 2020), several ratings went up nearly 2 percent nationally, and even more in two of the hottest Covid-19 hotspots at the time, Washington state (4.3 percent) and New York (13.2 percent). Ratings of the skill of physicians rose 2.4 percent nationally, 2.8 percent in Washington, and 10.4 percent in New York. Ratings of nursing rose 2.4 percent, 2.5 percent, and 10.4 percent, respectively. Pain control ratings improved 2.9 percent, 5.4 percent, and 12.5 percent, respectively.

The only measure of human interaction that did not go up was "Staff attitude toward visitors." That fell 0.7 percent nationally and 1.7 percent in Washington, but even that measure rose 6.1 percent in New York. Our interpretation is that the personnel in those hard-hit institutions were making authentic efforts to show their concern for patients' families, and their work was appreciated.

The data had a dark side, too. The surveys showed that patients' ratings of the cleanliness of hospital environments fell 2.2 percent nationally from February to March. (Declines were 4 percent in Washington and 2.5 percent in New York.) This finding suggested that patients everywhere were increasingly unnerved as the weeks went by, and two forces were influencing the amount of trust patients felt in their healthcare: their appreciation for the efforts of healthcare personnel pushed trust up, but their anxiety about the dangers of Covid-19 pushed it down.

Patients' trust in their healthcare providers is dynamic—it can go up and it can go down, and it did both in the early years of the Covid-19 pandemic. As time and the pandemic wore on, patient-experience ratings began to decline in every region and in all aspects of healthcare. There are probably several causes of the decline, including staffing shortages and the growing weariness of both patients and caregivers.

Earning Trust Among Caregivers

The dynamic nature of trust has been evident in the healthcare workforce, too. In this case, the rise and the decline happened simultaneously, bringing both good news and bad news at many institutions. From the start, it was clear that people working in healthcare were proud to be doing what they did, but they also felt vulnerable and under duress. Survey data showed that stresses were particularly great among frontline caregivers in the emergency departments and intensive care units—nurses and doctors, technicians, and other personnel who are essential in managing ventilators and medications.

While visibility of leadership during in-person walk rounds was important for building trust, it wasn't enough on its own. Table 2.1 shows how a wide range of situations could have either negative or positive impacts on workforce trust. And in many organizations both positive and negative impacts were apparent in these areas at the same time.

Table 2.1 Impact of Covid-19 on Trust Among the Workforce

Source of Impact	Negative Impact	Positive Impact
Resources	Caregivers felt unsafe due to a real or perceived lack of resources, PPE, testing, and equipment during the pandemic.	Caregivers felt well-protected with sufficient PPE and other resources.
Compensation	The organization furloughed and/or cut compensation for a portion of the workforce, leading to increased job insecurity.	Employees remained employed without loss of salary or benefits.
Staffing	Staffing shortages and/or staff redeployed outside their typical work environment created a sense of compromised safety.	Staff was supplemented by agency workers or with well-trained caregivers deployed from other departments.
Communication	Employees and medical staff perceived a disconnect between the communication from leaders and what happened at the bedside.	Reliable communication was seen as a "source of truth," and there was an opportunity for frontline workers to engage with leaders, ask questions, and influence change.
Transparency	A perceived lack of transparency about risks, protections, and work status diminished trust in leadership.	Transparency about institutional, citywide, statewide, and federal actions increased the sense of candor.
Increased Stress	Employees, medical staff, and leaders displayed signs of burnout—emotional exhaustion and depersonalization.	The workforce was fully engaged, fired up, and ready to go, taking pride in being on the front lines.

(continued)

(continued)

Source of Impact	Negative Impact	Positive Impact
Behavioral Health	Anxiety, depression, and post-traumatic stress disorder (PTSD) were not addressed or supported with resources.	Mental health needs were acknowledged, and proactively addressed and supported without stigma.

Early in the pandemic, Jessica Dudley, Press Ganey's chief clinical officer, created a collaborative among clinical leaders at client organizations that met weekly to share experiences and best practices. For leaders at many organizations, a key early lesson was that *all* of the areas in Table 2.1 warranted attention, and that no one should assume that effective efforts addressing just one or two could put the issue of workforce trust to rest.

Leaders developed communication strategies to deliver a unified source of information and created channels for staff to share concerns and for leaders to respond. (We believe that the special efforts given to communication help explain why median physician engagement improved from 2020 to 2021, despite the tremendous stress on clinicians.) While resources were often scarce, the creativity that caregivers demonstrated in solving challenges was remarkable. Organizations demonstrated agility in increasing ICU capacity, creating new staffing models with redeployed employees, and adopting new care models, such as telemedicine.

There was a strong sense that the crisis was bringing out the best in individuals and the organizations themselves, and both were aspiring to make those positive developments permanent. However, there were also concerns that once the crisis was over, the reasons for being at one's best would fade away. Financial stress might preempt efforts to organize care around patients' needs and support caregivers.

Table 2.2 groups trust-building practices described during Press Ganey's Covid-19 collaboratives into Frances Frei's three categories of authenticity, logic, and empathy.

Table 2.2 How Organizations Built Trust During the Initial Covid-19 Surge

Component of Trust	Trust-Building Activity
Authenticity	• Visible leadership rounding, asking how people are doing • Clear, concise communications • Transparency on metrics, planning

Logic	• Incident command structures, daily problem solving
	• Visible planning for process, physical resources, and personnel resources
	• Establishing Covid-19 units
	• Sourcing PPE and ventilators
	• Processes for conserving PPE
	• Creating new staffing models
	   ○ Redeploying furloughed staff for new roles
	   ○ Leader succession planning in case of illness
	• Maintaining communication regarding metrics, capacity, and planning
	• Visible evidence of safety practices to protect staff (e.g., screening for staff and community, availability of PPE)
	• Streamlining work (e.g., anterooms to don/doff PPE to make more efficient and reduce worry over fidelity to standards)
	• Removing barriers to doing the job (e.g., instituting telemedicine, IRB approval within hours)
	• Conducting pulse surveys to assess needs and supports for staff on the front line

(continued)

(continued)

Component of Trust	Trust-Building Activity

Empathy	• Hotels/dorms to house staff to prevent infection of family
	• Provision of scrubs/showers prior to leaving
	• Convenience services (food at work, grocery delivery)
	• Addressing hardships (e.g., sharing of healthcare costs for furloughed staff)
	• Communicating successful numbers of extubations, numbers of discharges
	• Celebrating clinical success (songs for extubations, clapping patients out of ICU, songs for Covid-19 discharges)
	• Debriefs post code
	• Code Lavender
	• Community appreciation/media
	• Real and virtual kudo boards/positive comments
	• Virtual post-shift debriefs to support staff
	• Resilience promotion
	  ○ Oasis rooms
	  ○ Caregiver checklist to leave
	  ○ Wellness buddy program
	  ○ Psych/behavioral health professionals and chaplains deployed to staff in their work environment
	  ○ Mental-health rounding
	  ○ Drop-in counseling
	  ○ Town halls on stress
	  ○ Guided meditations
	  ○ Instituting/augmenting peer support
	  ○ Acknowledging likelihood of PTSD, proactively working to prevent it rather than waiting for it to develop

Safety

When Covid-19 arrived, the immediate concern was the physical safety of patients and of the people taking care of them in emergency departments and hospitals. The initial focus was on the risk of coronavirus infection, but it quickly broadened to include other types of harm and other settings for care.

Measures like mask-wearing and distancing were highly effective in preventing the spread of Covid-19 among patients and caregivers—but not perfectly so. At many hospitals, there were outbreaks like the widely publicized one at Brigham and Women's Hospital in Boston (where I do my clinical work), which affected 42 employees and 15 patients in September 2020. Detailed contact tracing and comprehensive testing on 7,999 employees identified several causes, including inconsistencies in patient masking, the failure to use eye protection among providers, and a lack of physical distancing among staff when eating.[3]

Outbreaks like the one at Brigham's were so rare they could be intensively studied—and that meant preventive measures were actually working remarkably well. Doctors, nurses, and respiratory technicians who were working 8 to 12 hours a day with patients who were severely ill with Covid-19 usually did not get infected themselves—and when they did, it turned out that, more often than not, they were exposed outside of the workplace.

While the spread of Covid-19 was surprisingly well contained in the initial phases of the pandemic, other types of safety events increased across every type of hospital unit: adult critical care, medical, step-down, high quality, moderate acuity, surgical, and so on. For example, there was a national rise in the rate of central line-associated blood stream infections (CLABSIs), which presumably reflected difficulty changing lines when patients are intubated and in a prone position. Pressure ulcers increased, too.

Some of the safety events were only indirectly related to Covid-19, but still caused by the pandemic. For example, there was an increase in falls, probably due in part to exclusion of family members because of restrictions on visitors. In a common scenario, an elderly patient, alone in their room, falls while trying to get up to go to the bathroom without assistance.

At Press Ganey, we saw a deterioration in measures of safety culture around the country, and our nursing quality data captured rising rates of adverse events. As tempers frayed and people became exhausted, nurses and other caregivers quit their jobs or retired early, exacerbating staffing problems that were already severe because so many employees were in quarantine. Stress on the workforce was also worsened by incidents in which patients and families assaulted nurses and other caregivers over issues such as masking mandates, visitation policies, vaccine recommendations, and use of unapproved therapies like ivermectin.

Physical harm was just one type of injury that posed challenges for healthcare organizations as the impact of the pandemic and growing concern over DEI broadened the definition of *harm*. Organizations came to recognize the importance of emotional and psychological harm (e.g., fear, burnout, even suicide), sociobehavioral harm (e.g., feeling disrespected or not credible), and financial harm (e.g., loss of income or exposure to unexpected costs).[4]

When vaccines became available at the end of 2020, organizations had to implement programs to vaccinate their employees with the goal of keeping them safe. They had to make decisions about who would get immunized first, how to communicate the availability and administration of vaccinations, and how to coordinate the scheduling of immunizations. (Considering the side effects, organizations often staggered the scheduling of frontline workers to reduce the chances that multiple people with the same job would be unable to work at the same time.)

At Geisinger Health System, for example, the vaccination program for employees was planned in detail well in advance of the FDA's Emergency Use Authorization for the Pfizer-BioNTech vaccine on December 11, 2020.[5] The first vaccinations were administered on December 17, prioritizing frontline clinicians with the most significant and consistent exposure. Within two months, more than 60 percent of the workforce was vaccinated and positive test rates among employees were falling. By March 15, 2021, 68 percent of employees were vaccinated.[6]

Then, a new problem arose. Many of the remaining staff were hesitant about getting vaccinated. And for much of the rest of 2021, Geisinger and virtually every other healthcare organization was consumed with the questions of whether and how to implement a vaccine mandate.

Houston Methodist was the first major organization to announce that vaccination was mandatory for employees who did not have a medical or religious reason for exemption. Its leadership was greeted with protests and lawsuits, as well as the thanks of employees who were not happy about being exposed to unvaccinated coworkers. And ultimately, most healthcare organizations followed suit. In essentially every instance, the argument was the same—safety.

Equity

As they did with safety, healthcare organizations broadened and deepened their understanding of the challenges of improving the diversity, equity, and inclusion (DEI) of their care and their cultures. Broadening meant that organizations realized that DEI was an issue that was not limited to underrepresented minorities defined by race and ethnicity. It was also an important cause of discontent for women, Asians, and people with disabilities.

For example, a cross-sectional study of nearly 65 million patients across 547 healthcare organizations showed that having an intellectual disability was the strongest independent risk factor for a Covid-19 diagnosis, and the strongest independent risk factor other than age for mortality due to Covid-19. These data made a strong argument that screening for Covid-19, care coordination, and vaccination efforts should be especially intense within this population and for their caregivers, as these patients are less able to consistently use masks and socially distance.[7]

This example shows the importance of a change in the perspective of healthcare providers who might once have thought that equitable care meant treating everyone the same. In some ways, that is true—equitable care means treating every patient as an individual, assessing their needs, and doing all that is possible to meet them. But equitable care is not doing the same thing for everyone; it is tailoring care to the needs of every individual. It is patient-centered care delivered with high reliability.

Healthcare professionals had an epiphany as they considered the implications of Covid-19 and the surge of concern about DEI. Instead of considering safety, equity, technical quality, public health, patient experience, and workforce well-being as separate issues, they all were parts of the same work. Approaching that work with high reliability was a recipe for the secret sauce of excellence.

In January 2020, Karthik Sivashanker and Tejal Gandhi published an eloquent argument in *The New England Journal of Medicine*. Their thesis: there is no such thing as high-quality, safe care that is inequitable; addressing inequity in healthcare requires a systems-based approach akin to those used in safety.[8]

In an analogous development, healthcare organizations found that they could not really meet staffing challenges without meaningful progress on diversity, equity, and inclusion. As I noted in Chapter 1, data demonstrated that DEI is strongly correlated with employees' stated likelihood of leaving. This relationship cuts across every job type.

Common sense was borne out by ample data in a survey of 410,000 employees in 2021. When employees of all types rated their organizations above the median for diversity and equity among employees, they were much less likely to suggest that they would leave. When people feel like they belong at an organization, they are less likely to be looking for the door.

Another key insight regarding equity in the workforce was analogous to insights about segmenting and personalizing care for patients; organizations began to understand that one size does not fit all when it came to their employees, too. For example, when women physicians began to report higher levels of burnout and of cutting back or quitting their jobs, the special needs of women physicians, who tended to bear the brunt of the responsibility for addressing problems posed by the pandemic in family life, began to get more attention.

My colleague Jessica Dudley made a detailed analysis of Press Ganey data that showed that physicians of different genders find similar degrees of meaning in their work, but that women are less likely to leave work behind and give themselves a chance to recover. Her data also showed that women physicians are less likely to believe that their organization values and demonstrates a commitment to diversity than are their male counterparts of the same racial or ethnic background.[9]

Again, the answer is not to be "color-blind" or "gender-blind" and treat everyone the same. The approach to helping women in general—and female physicians in particular—to stay in the workforce should include an array of interventions, many of which should be tailored to specific groups of women. For example, the demands on a working mother with school-aged children are different than those on a working woman in her 50s or 60s who has aging parents.

The demands on different subsets of the patient population and the workforce have always been there, but Covid-19 was the stress test that brought them to a crisis level. The leaders of many healthcare organizations realized that good intentions were not enough. They had to manage these challenges the way they managed other work—by gathering data, identifying problems, and developing, evaluating, and improving strategies.

Safety-net institutions had another key insight—they could not take on equity issues for their patients using their own data and resources; they had to collaborate and integrate with public health systems. Physicians in Bergamo, the epicenter of the Covid-19 outbreak in Italy, made a broader observation in the first brutal weeks of the pandemic. They wrote that "in a pandemic, patient-centered care is inadequate and must be replaced by community-centered care. Solutions for Covid-19 are required for the entire population, not just for hospitals."[10]

That is the kind of clarity that comes from having one's back to the wall, knowing that business-as-usual is not working. And that same sense of determination led the leaders of Parkland Health and Hospital System to rethink their roles in care delivery, and then integrate their work with other healthcare and public health leaders in Dallas, Texas. They began working together on public health functions of collecting and analyzing data, contact tracing, outbreak investigation, immunizations, isolation, quarantine, and social services support. Technology-based solutions were deployed to identify people most at risk of exposure to Covid-19. Parkland's Center for Clinical Innovations developed a Social Needs Index, a Proximity Index, and a Vulnerability Index to identify and care for the county's high-risk population, drawing on detailed information about social issues relevant to the neighborhoods in which people lived.[11]

Consumerism

At the annual J.P. Morgan Healthcare Conference in January 2020— a time that seems so innocent today—the leaders of large healthcare systems paraded to the stage for 45-minute presentations describing their current business outlooks and their strategies for growth. The concept of consumerism was brought up constantly, and several speakers displayed working prototypes of smartphone apps that allowed patients to get test results, ask questions, and even book appointments. The goal was "stickiness"—making it easier for patients to interact with their organizations so that they would be less likely to leave.

A few years later, many of those healthcare organizations have had to devote most of their attention to immediate crises, like staffing their emergency departments and patient care units, and keeping their patients and employees safe. Part of that effort was supporting telemedicine, which surged to unprecedented levels in almost every organization in the first half of 2020, and then settled out at about 10 to 15 percent of outpatient interactions.

But organizations have varied markedly in the extent to which they have invested in telemedicine as part of the future. Many have provided little coaching for physicians and the rest of the care delivery team on how to make telemedicine work for patients, while others have made major commitments.

At Weill Cornell Medical College, for example, telemedicine training has become part of the core curriculum for all students. "Physicians and clinical providers are responsible for creating a safe personal connection with the patients through a screen, and not all of them have the skill set to do so," Rahul Sharma, MD, the program's leader told me in an interview. "When this pandemic started, people thought it was easy, but I will tell you that doing a virtual visit, telemedicine visit, with a patient is not the same as Faceting with your grandparents or your friend. There is a skill set that you need to do this."[12]

Sharma went on to describe some of the most common errors, such as not looking at the camera, making poor eye contact, or not taking any steps to convey empathy over the video screen. The curriculum that he developed teaches the equivalent of a good bedside manner, while also sharing steps for a reasonable physical examination. The reception among staff and trainees has been quite positive, presumably because everyone who has done virtual visits recognizes that they have plenty of room for improvement.

Press Ganey data show that, from the start, patients have appreciated the efforts of clinicians. The ratings for care providers are similar for both in-person and virtual visits, but there is a sizeable gap in patients' overall likelihood of recommending the practice. Patients who completed a survey after virtual visits were less likely to recommend the practice than those who completed it after seeing the physician in person. However, that gap appears to be narrowing, reflecting focused work in organizations that grasp that telemedicine is here to stay.

The acceptance of telemedicine is only one example of people's increasing willingness to make choices that are not dominated by brand loyalty. As healthcare organizations have seen, brand loyalty is becoming less effective in helping them retain their workforces or their patients, who are increasingly ready to get their needs met wherever, whenever they can.

This readiness to look outside of traditional healthcare providers' offices was essential in convincing patients to be tested and vaccinated for Covid-19. I have consistently told my patients that they shouldn't think of my primary care center as the place to get these things done; they should go to their local pharmacy. We simply didn't have the supplies or the personnel to deliver these services, and the pharmacies did.

Sending patients out into the world to get Covid-19 care was the right thing to do for them and for public health, but it was also an acknowledgment that patients are going to get their needs met in a much wider range of ways than in the past. That is why there has been a surge in investments in new companies providing services that will meet patients' needs outside the traditional healthcare system. It is also why large companies like CVS and Amazon are taking steps to become major forces in primary care and other parts of medicine.

Some healthcare organizations, driven by new competition or out of necessity, are redesigning how they deliver digital care. Sanford Health, a large rural health system across North and South Dakota, Minnesota, and Iowa, received a $350 million gift in September 2021 to reimagine how it delivered care across the vast distances where its patients live. Sanford is moving beyond conventional telehealth platforms to create a true virtual care center that enables primary care, remote home monitoring, and ICU care, along with direct access to specialists and behavioral health resources. There will be five fully integrated rural satellite clinics for communities of 2,000 or less or in areas where no care options currently exist. These will be 1,000-square-foot facilities with two exam rooms staffed by registered nurses who have direct access to clinicians in the virtual care center.

It seems likely that innovations from rural care, where distances pose truly substantial barriers to in-person care, will make their way into the rest of healthcare as consumers in cities also realize that they don't really want to spend hours traveling or waiting to see their clinicians.

Marketplace Changes

In addition to greater collaboration between providers and payers on managed Medicare, the Covid-19 pandemic produced more radical innovations, some by organizations that were already integrated payer-providers. For example, Kaiser Permanente and Spectrum (now Corewell) Health in Michigan introduced "Telehealth First" insurance products, in which patients would have no co-pay if they first sought care for problems through telehealth options. These insurance products were priced up to 20 percent lower than traditional products in the communities they served.[13] Teladoc and other nontraditional healthcare organizations employ the same basic approach—starting the care episode with a virtual primary- or urgent-care visit.

Such innovations suggest that while many traditional healthcare providers may look at telemedicine as a new wrinkle to be accommodated, the new entrants—and some forward-looking traditional organizations—see telemedicine differently. They view it as an innovation that is both disruptive—a simpler solution for patients with simpler needs or for patients who are currently not being served—and sustaining—one that yields incremental improvements to what is already being done for patients.[14] While the percentage of patients using telemedicine from nontraditional healthcare providers might have seemed small enough to ignore at the beginning of the current decade, no one doubts that it will be much higher by the end.

The pandemic also showed how integrated payer-provider organizations could be nimble in responding to patients' needs. For example, Oak Street Health, a network of primary care centers providing high-touch, value-based medical care for adults on Medicare, quickly focused on helping patients stay at home as much as possible. In the first few weeks of the pandemic, Oak Street developed a remote care program that allowed them to perform 93 percent of visits by phone or video. It reoriented its transportation system, which had been developed to help get patients to the clinics, to fulfill the opposite goal—helping them stay at home. Instead of transporting patients, the system was used to deliver food and medications so seniors could reduce their Covid-19 exposure. This organization and other innovative primary care organizations helped define the possibilities of value-based models that allow providers to focus not on what is being reimbursed, but on what patients need.[15]

Stepping back from the responses to these individual big-picture challenges—trust, safety, equity, consumerism, and market-place changes—many organizations understood that there was an even bigger challenge that helped define their ability to respond to the crisis of the moment—adopting the principles of highly reliable organizations. As one who has observed a wide range of organizations across healthcare, I have the impression that those who had been working for years on developing a high-reliability culture fared better during the early years of this decade.

Houston Methodist, for example, has had to deal with the Covid-19 and equity concerns like every other US healthcare organization, but it has also faced tropical storms, electrical grid failures, and crushing heat waves. Its leaders believe strongly that their work to incorporate high-reliability principles related to safety and quality was critical for their ability to respond to more recent crises. They wrote: "At Houston Methodist, our focus for the past decade has been to become an HRO and a learning healthcare system where we can safely perform our normal work on a daily basis and seamlessly shift into disaster mode, when necessary, without sacrificing the quality of care for our patients or the well-being of our employees."[16]

During the Covid-19 pandemic, they were able to develop a program to safely provide surgical care with a low risk of Covid-19 infection for patients. Data on 141,439 patients who underwent surgery from March 1, 2020, to September 30, 2021, found an overall Covid-19 infection rate of 0.6 percent. Detailed analyses of data from patients who had Covid-19 after their risk-reduction program was put in place showed that most probably had contracted the disease from community sources, so that the true nosocomial infection rate was about 0.1 percent.[17]

Houston Methodist has embraced the goal of becoming a learning system that is constantly trying to get better, and a resilient system that can adapt to disasters without compromising its commitment to values. It was far from the only organization that found the principles of high reliability to be critical in managing the challenges of the pandemic. RWJBarnabas Health and Ochsner Health are among several others with similar stories to tell. Part II of this book will explore what it takes to become a resilient system that can adapt to disasters without sacrificing excellence.

PART II

THE ROAD AHEAD

CHAPTER 3

Enduring Challenges

HEALTHCARE HAS CHANGED, and there is no going back. Both patients and the workforce are different than they were just a few years ago. The ways in which people interact with healthcare have changed, and the units of analysis for episodes of care that matter most are defined by what patients are experiencing rather than what generates relative value units for billing purposes. The workings of the healthcare marketplace are lagging behind the evolution of care delivery, but only a little; the marketplace is changing rapidly, too.

These changes were underway before 2020, but have accelerated in the last few years, making adaptation more compelling and more urgent. In addition to adapting to recent changes, organizations must prepare for a future in which major disruptions can occur at any time. During times of turmoil, they must be able to preserve excellence and maintain the trust of their patients and employees.

We can anticipate four major types of enduring challenges in the next few years: changes in patients, in the unit of analysis defining care, in the workforce, and in the market.

Changes in Patients

While the Covid-19 pandemic has recently dominated health-care and highlighted the importance of trust, there are at least two durable trends that make trust a critical long-term focus for organizations in the industry. Both of these trends are dynamic forces that will give new meaning and importance to patient-centered care in the years ahead.

The first trend deepens the meaning of patient-centered care. It is the evolving nature of concerns about diversity, equity, and inclusion (DEI). These concerns are relevant to groups defined by race, ethnicity, gender, abilities, body habitus, and a range of other issues. All patients are concerned about the fairness and effectiveness with which their needs are being met. Progress in DEI is not defined by the goal of treating everyone the same, but on treating everyone as an individual whose concerns are considered credible and whose needs are taken seriously.

In a sense, DEI has become a high-reliability focus—and respect is becoming just as important as safety. Respect is a fundamental element in every interaction with every patient. Just as the only safety goal that makes sense is zero harm, the only goals for DEI that make sense are zero inequity and zero disrespect.

This represents an expansion of the concept of excellence for many clinicians, and that makes perfect sense. Care cannot be considered excellent or successful unless patients have peace of mind. To achieve that, they must believe that *they* are believed, that their needs are being recognized, that their suffering is appreciated, and that every effort is being made on their behalf.

I think almost every clinician knows how to deliver that kind of care for the patients with whom they identify, for example when seeing the family member of a colleague. But high-reliability DEI demands the clinicians be at their best with every single patient, including the many with whom they do not readily identify. This progress will require creating new social norms within healthcare.

The other powerful trend—the one that underscores the importance of patient-centered care—is the aging of the baby boomer generation. The wave of people born after the end of World War II has transformed every American institution it passed through, including education, marriage, parenthood, work, and retirement. Boomers are now in their 60s or beyond, and there is every reason to expect that they will have profound effects on healthcare, too.

As the baby boomers age, they are living with chronic conditions like diabetes and hypertension, having surgery on their joints, and developing heart disease and cancers. They are not a group known for stoicism or accepting their fates. They have high expectations for their healthcare. They want excellence. They want convenience. They want to trust their clinicians. They also want autonomy.

One of my colleagues had an ablation for recurrent atrial fibrillation right before the winter holidays in 2021, and his experience illuminates the challenge boomers pose as patients. First the good news: the procedure itself went smoothly, with no complications. As a result, the risk of future episodes in which his heart races in rapid, irregular patterns is greatly reduced. If all goes well, he might not need medication to slow his heart or prevent blood clot formation.

The other good news is that major elements of the procedure were just what the patient wanted. It was performed by a respected physician who was deeply experienced in this procedure, which is still relatively new. It was performed at a highly respected hospital with plenty of backup in case complications developed. The patient had to wait only a few weeks for the procedure instead of several months, because a cancelation created an opening in the schedule right before Christmas.

The patient is grateful for all the above—and, as a clinician, my instinctive reaction is, "Hey, things went well! What's not to like?" But, from the perspective of the patient, several issues compromised trust:

- He made the decision that the benefits of an invasive procedure exceeded the risks, but then learned that the wait for the procedure would be six months, which made him wonder whether his healthcare team viewed his problems as important.

- The pre-procedure logistics were compressed by the change in scheduling, but they became chaotic because they involved multiple telephone calls from various people involved in the patient's care. Like many people today who have been overwhelmed with spam calls, the patient had stopped answering his phone unless he recognized the number. As a result, he learned just one day in advance that his care team had scheduled a CT angiogram to map out his pulmonary vasculature, and he was out of state at the time of the appointment. His is just one of many examples of chaos resulting from multiple ways in which people communicate today, with none of them completely reliable. This is a problem that is just being recognized in healthcare, and it is far from solved.

- Ideally, the patient would have had a single point of contact, but instead he had several. Sometimes, their choice of words raised questions in his mind about whether his care providers were working together closely or if they knew what was going to happen next. He also overheard physicians talking about whether they could bill for certain procedures, which was not what he hoped they would be focusing on at the moment. (He was lying on a stretcher nearby.)

- When the procedure was over and he was discharged, he was given a printout of warning signs of complications, but no one called him to check on him. In fact, he didn't speak in person to the physician who did the procedure, either before or afterward.

My colleague knows he was fortunate to have an expert at a good hospital perform the procedure just days before elective surgeries associated with overnight stays were paused by the Omicron surge. But the fact remains—even though the procedure went well technically, his care could have been better.

If there were an after-action review of his case, the conclusion would be that a good clinical outcome was achieved, despite considerable logistical challenges. But there are a couple of important lessons to be learned.

First, we need better ways of communicating with patients. Since the telephone is becoming increasingly unreliable, a single person, whose name and phone number are recognizable to the patient, should coordinate all care. That would reduce the anxiety caused by wondering whether the caregivers were working as a team.

Second, everyone involved in the patient's care should understand that, when they are in the presence of the patient, they should assume that the patient hears everything they say. This would be an incentive for them to behave as patients would hope and expect.

Changes in the Unit of Analysis Defining Care

In addition to changes in the patient population, there is a change underway in units of analysis defining care. Patients don't think in terms of the units that are reimbursed under fee-for-service models. They think in terms of the episodes of care. Healthcare organizations seeking to earn patients' trust must orient their performance around the same units of analysis.

For patients with chronic conditions like hypertension, diabetes, and high cholesterol, the episodes are long in duration, and even indefinite. In-person doctor visits are not the units of analysis that matter most to patients; instead, they think about how the relationship has gone over the past year or so. Thus, non-visit interactions can be more important in defining the patient's perspective than face-to-face contact.

To grasp the meaning of thinking in terms of the episodes that matter to patients, it is worth watching the famous TED talk by Daniel Kahneman, the Nobel-laureate psychologist, on the difference between memory and experience.[1]

Kahneman describes how memories are shaped by "peaks and ends"—that is, the extreme positive and negative moments of the episode, and the final stretch. While his talk does not address healthcare directly, it conveys a message that our job as healthcare providers is something more than being wonderful during as many of our interactions as possible. Instead, our job is be "producer-director" and shape a positive memory for patients about what happened during their episode of care.

The goal, of course, is not to trick the patient into thinking that they had a great episode of care. The goal is to ensure that they have a great episode. That is how a great memory is created—the work is nothing less than that. Caregivers should imagine how patients ideally might describe their care to others, then work to make that ideal vision real.

Delivering ideal care takes more work than providing good visits, but it also has greater benefits for the caregivers themselves. It makes caregivers proud and makes them want to stay where they are. Overall, the challenge of empathizing with patients and adopting their units of analysis is good business strategy. Still, this shift is a change from business as usual. For an acute problem like joint pain or an itchy rash, the episode begins when the patient becomes aware of the issue and starts seeking help. Often, that search starts when patients look up their symptoms online and search for doctors or organizations that might be able to help them.

For problems that are acute on chronic—such as worsening shortness of breath for patients with known heart disease, or a loss of appetite for someone with a cancer history—they are likely to have a combination of the two perspectives. They will be thinking not only about how their care has been over the past few months and years, but also how smoothly their search for help with new manifestations of their condition has gone.

In these contexts, the manner in which physicians conduct themselves when face to face with patients really matters, of course. Press Ganey's data in every setting of care show that patients care deeply about whether their clinician—especially doctors and nurses—shows empathy, communicates well, and coordinates effectively with other clinicians. These characteristics of care are much more important drivers of patient loyalty than wait times or how well pain is controlled. More recent data show that the success of face-to-face interactions is not the only driver of patient loyalty. All the things that happen throughout the entire episode of care influence patients' trust and loyalty, and that is reflected in their likelihood to recommend the caregiver or the facility. Forward-looking healthcare providers should consider the entire episode of care as an opportunity to win their patients' loyalty and build their trust.

Ample data demonstrate the importance of measuring and trying to improve what happens to patients before they even walk in the door for a visit—and the findings are apparent in every organization my colleagues at Press Ganey have surveyed. In these analyses, patients are separated into two groups based on whether or not they had friction—difficulty in reaching the practice, getting an appointment in a timely manner, or getting information about delays—before the visit.

When patients had a smooth course before the visit, they tended to give the practice very high ratings in terms of likelihood to recommend. But when patients had pre-visit friction, the ratings were low. What varies widely is the proportion of patients who report friction before the visit; it can be as low as 20 percent and as high as 75 percent in the analyses I have reviewed. But even for the great practices where the rate of problems is just 20 percent, there is plenty of room for improvement. Patients want what we all want—a smooth set of processes surrounding potentially difficult discussions about their health.

I know this from personal experience. I was supposed to have an eye appointment—a six-month follow-up after a minor procedure—on December 28, 2021. I had booked the appointment during the holidays so that it would not interfere with my work. A month beforehand, I got a letter telling me the visit was canceled, and that I should call the office to book a new one. I don't know the details, but I assumed that the physician (whom I like a lot) realized that she was booked for sessions during the holidays and canceled them.

I called the number and was on hold for 20 minutes before I had to give up to attend a meeting. I called back later, when I had a full hour between meetings, so that I could work at my computer while waiting on hold for the scheduler. After another 20 minutes, I finally scheduled an appointment for February.

I wasn't harmed by having to call back twice and waiting so long. I sat at my desk and worked, as I likely would have done anyway. But if you can imagine listening to their recorded music loop endlessly, you can probably understand why I consider this pre-visit episode to have friction.

This experience brought to mind a comment made several years ago by a highly respected physician at a major urban teaching hospital not far from my own. He told me how one of his patients said, "Every step of the process before I get in the door to see you is like hacking my way through a jungle. Getting the appointment, parking, fighting my way through the registration system—it's all terrible. But then I get in the door, and sit across from you, and I feel like it was all worth it."

The point that this physician was making to me was that what *he* did was what really mattered in healthcare. And he *was* wonderful; he gave every patient his complete attention, and they felt it and appreciated it. He was among the most respected physicians in the world in his specialty, and patients knew it; they left with peace of mind that they could not have seen anyone more expert. But his attitude implied that the other aspects of the experience were not that important. I was relatively new to management at that time, but even then I understood that, at some level, he might have unconsciously liked the idea of being the hero who made the dysfunctional system worthwhile. In any case, he didn't worry much about what happened before or after; he didn't think it had anything to do with his personal excellence.

As patient expectations have changed, these pre- and post-visit experiences have become more important. If, as always, physicians need to focus on delivering positive direct interactions with patients, the organizations to which they belong must take responsibility for the overall episode of care. If they don't, they should expect an erosion of trust. Patients today know that medicine is a team sport and that what their personal physicians do and say is not the only thing that matters. When there is dysfunction in the processes that surround physicians, patients must wonder, "What else aren't they getting right?"

Beyond thinking more broadly about the episodes of care that matter to patients, healthcare organizations must also think beyond the traditional doctor-patient relationship. Because of the complexity of medical problems and social situations that come with advanced age, the individual patient is often no longer the total unit of analysis. In fact, as patients get into their late 80s and 90s, it is extremely common for family members to be deeply involved in their care. As a result, the effectiveness of the team-family relationship is often what determines how successfully a patient's needs can be met.

Changes in the Workforce

The enormous challenge of recruiting and retaining doctors and nurses has been front-page news during the pandemic. Less attention has been given to changes affecting the rest of the healthcare workforce. In reality, *all* types of personnel have been in short supply, and the related staffing problems have caused major issues for healthcare organizations. In the years ahead, organizations will need new approaches to deal with changes in the workforce.

Retaining all types of employees will be a constant struggle for the foreseeable future. On one hand, data demonstrate that every type of employee in healthcare—from clinicians to security guards and back-office staff—takes pride in the nature of their work. On the other, their loyalty to individual organizations is lower than in the past. They are more open to considering other opportunities, and they are ready to move on when a more attractive position becomes available.

As organizations vie for employees, competition is actually greater at the lower end of the pay scale. More businesses around the country have implemented minimum wage levels of $15 per hour or more. The result is that healthcare organizations are losing employees to supermarkets, fast-food franchises, Amazon warehouses, and other businesses that would have been unlikely competitors in the past. As of late May 2022, an ice cream store near where I live in Boston was hiring scoopers at $17.50 to $22.00 per hour. Who wouldn't consider a job change that raised one's income by one-third?

The competition for employees is further complicated for healthcare organizations because of the constant change in required skills. Because today's organizational charts were developed to deliver yesterday's healthcare, no organization will have the exact people in place to perform the work that is immediately needed. When crises like the pandemic arise, the mismatch between the available workforce and the needed workforce is even greater.

Change is constant, so workforces must be hired and trained for change. The implication is that resilience and flexibility must be built into human-resource planning. One way to deal with new needs is to hire new people. Another is to use temporary personnel brought in through agencies, which is expensive and disruptive, but often necessary. Still another is to build job descriptions that are adaptable, flexible, and resilient, and to implement routine cross-training so that employees take on different roles.

The growing diversity of the workforce will make it essential to have an inclusive organizational culture. The fact is that virtually everyone who is not a white male is an underrepresented minority in healthcare C-suites, but women and minorities constitute the majority—often a dominant majority—of every type of employee. Managers should be constantly asking the question: does everyone on our staff feel like they belong here?

There is no simple response to that simple question; no single step makes an organization a good place for women to work. Every group—whether based on gender, ethnicity, religion, or numerous other identifiers—is heterogeneous, made up of individuals with different needs and expectations.

For example, Asians don't think of themselves as *Asian*; they think of themselves as people who came from China or Vietnam or India or America or whatever their country of origin might be. In this context, a one-size-fits-all approach, like celebrating Asian-American Day, is likely to cause amusement or offense, even if intentions are good.

The gap in workforce diversity is greatest in the senior management teams of healthcare, and differences are widening. Women now constitute the majority of medical school graduates, and the percentages of various types of employees who self-identify as non-white continues to rise. Organizations that hope to recruit and retain these employees must make them feel that they are welcome and belong.

Changes in the Market

As highlighted in the opening chapter, the pandemic caused many people to spend more time at home, staring at the screens of their computers or smartphones. They got used to finding information and meeting their needs through digital interactions. While many of them value the warmth of face-to-face interactions and are happy to return to in-person activities, they also like being able to stay home at their convenience and have digital options on demand.

Patients are no exception. Organizations won't meet this enduring challenge just by delivering excellent telehealth visits. They need to consider the full episode of care from the patient perspective—from the moment that they type their medical questions into Google and begin searching for a physician with the expertise to address them.

This new pattern disrupts the old model of the medical practice. In the past, healthcare organizations used a good brand to attract patients, and they were rewarded financially if those patients booked visits, tests, and procedures. No one wanted patients to have a miserable experience scheduling their appointments and getting through the door, but healthcare organizations did not incur significant financial penalties if exasperated patients walked away, as long as there were other patients in line to fill their spots.

Today, however, the issues related to the patient experience are more complex. If patients get fed up with the care itself or the processes around it, they may tweet disparaging comments, post videos, or write nasty reviews on third-party sites like Healthgrades and Vitals. When other patients do Google searches, those negative comments come up. Positive reviews come up too, and consistently positive information online can do more than attract patients; it can also build their trust in the care they are choosing.

Set aside for a moment the idea of the patient visit, and instead think in terms of the relationship between patients and their caregivers, and the memory patients are left with. The digital experience is critical to shaping both. In medical school I was taught to go out to the waiting area to greet every single patient, shake their hand, look in their eyes, smile, and thank them for coming in. Addressing the digital aspects of the patient experience is the logical extension of that.

Patients' expectations for digital experiences are variable and high. At the 2022 J.P. Morgan Healthcare Conference, organizations listed ambitious "design specifications" for the future, including:

- Immediate virtual responses to queries

- Anytime, anywhere access to care

- Same-day access to in-person care

- Online appointment booking

- On-time appointments

- One-time registration

- One bill

Meeting these design specifications requires more than building slick systems. The human beings at either end of the digital interactions make it difficult to simplify the processes that support the patient experience. (An example is the variability with which people screen their phone calls due to the proliferation of spam calls.) This means that healthcare organizations need multi-layered approaches to digital interactions so patients can interact with providers any way they wish—and providers must be reliable in responding, however the patient chooses to communicate.

In addition to digitization, the healthcare marketplace has been shaped by changes in its payment system and the structure. Many of these shifts were underway before Covid hit, but those trends have accelerated. The ramifications will play out over several years—but not several decades. Skeptics of the need for transformation have quieted down, as it has become clear that the healthcare system must meet the needs of patients across the episodes of care. Moreover, healthcare organizations must work in ways that matter to patients and use the technologies they prefer.

The two big changes that drive this imperative are the expansion of value-based payment and increasing vertical integration in which payers and providers become parts of the same organization. The percentage of revenue for healthcare providers from population-management contracts such as Medicare Advantage and Medicaid managed care continues to grow, and it has passed 30 percent.[2]

One of the strongest forms of commitment is for providers to start their own insurance plans, merge with insurers, or enter into contracts that align their interests around efficiency and quality. The percentage of physicians in independent private practices is now below 50 percent, and most newly trained physicians are taking jobs in which they are employed by hospitals, insurers, and other types of delivery systems. A generation ago, such physician roles were the exception; soon they will be the rule. The transition is underway to a healthcare system in which physicians work in organizations that are accountable for both the quality and the overall costs of care.

The challenge for healthcare organizations is not figuring out whether—or even when—this transition will occur. The challenge is navigating the transition. Healthcare organizations must reduce patient suffering while managing the challenges arising from changes in the population, changes in the units of analysis defining care, the digitalization of healthcare, and changes in the workforce and the marketplace. The next chapter will describe what we can do while pursuing excellence and building trust.

CHAPTER 4

The Long-Term Response to Change

LONG-TERM CHANGES DEMAND long-term responses—responses that are essential for healthcare organizations to thrive over time. The responses must also be robust enough to adapt to medium-term disruptions (e.g., the Covid-19 pandemic) and short-term chaos (e.g., weather-related events).

This chapter provides an overview of six key responses. Collectively, these responses constitute the value chain of activities, which are essential in pursuing excellence in the years ahead:

1. Building trust in patients

2. Building trust in the workforce

3. Deepening and broadening safety

4. Committing to diversity, equity, and inclusion (DEI)

5. Responding to consumerism

6. Responding to market change

These six activities are not analogous to items on a restaurant menu, from which one can pick the items that most suit one's mood. Each is a part of a greater whole; they work like links in a chain and reinforce each other. This chapter will discuss them as a group, and each of the chapters in Part III will explore one activity in depth.

Excellence will require committed efforts to improve in all six. To provide a framework for thinking about these individual activities and how they fit together, we will first describe how the Covid-19 pandemic has sharpened the concepts of strategy and value chains for healthcare organizations.

Strategy and Value Chains in Post–Covid-19 Healthcare

The Covid-19 pandemic demanded crisis-management responses from virtually every healthcare organization, and, as the pandemic wore on, the sustained pressures often led to deep discussions of strategy. Organizations under duress had to grapple with the question of what was most important to preserve, which naturally led them to consider two issues that lie at the core of healthcare strategy: (1) the value that the organization is going to produce for patients, and (2) how the organization is going to be different from its competitors.

Competing on price alone makes it difficult for organizations to achieve the financial margins they need to thrive, regardless of whether they are for-profit or nonprofit. Points of differentiation are essential if organizations are to avoid competing on price alone. To differentiate themselves, organizations need to think clearly about their value chains—the sets of activities required to deliver services and create value for customers. Value chains include essential activities that are performed by third parties.

Value chains became relevant during the Covid-19 pandemic because no organization on its own could meet all the needs of all their patients. Healthcare providers had to collaborate with other organizations, including those that were ordinarily their competitors, government agencies, insurance companies, and pharmacy chains. In aggregate, the healthcare industry rose to the occasion. The impact of the pandemic would have been much more severe if not for cooperation among these stakeholders.

Value-chain thinking is a marked deviation from business as usual in healthcare. Instead of concentrating solely on the activities for which they are paid, managers applying value-chain thinking focus on all the activities that are essential to meet the needs of patients. After they identify those activities, they turn their attention to determining the most effective and efficient ways to perform those activities.

The concept of value chains was first described by Michael Porter in his 1985 book *Competitive Advantage*.[1] Porter observed that value is rarely, if ever, created in complex work by doing one thing extremely well. Instead, a *series* of activities is required to create value for customers. Successful strategies require a grasp of *all* the activities required to create value, with management ensuring that all are being performed with effectiveness and efficiency.

For example, effective Covid-19 vaccination campaigns began with research, clinical trials, and manufacturing efforts. Other key activities included developing distribution systems, public education, administration models, and follow-up surveillance. Failures in any activity compromise the impact of all of them.

For complex pursuits such as healthcare, these activities are inevitably intertwined. They do not necessarily occur in the same sequence for every patient, but they *must* occur, ideally concurrently. This approach forces managers to look beyond the boundaries of their own units or their own job descriptions, and see themselves as part of a larger system. Managing interdependencies becomes as important as managing within the organization's walls.

The following sections describe key activities that are part of the value chain for healthcare organizations that are seeking to deliver excellent care in the context of unexpected challenges.

Building Trust Among Patients

Trust is a form of social capital that may seem difficult to measure, but doing so should be an explicit focus for healthcare leaders and clinicians in the years ahead. The most direct way to assess whether patients trust their healthcare providers is to ask them. Because the word *trust* has variable interpretations, we usually use surrogate questions, like asking patients about their likelihood of recommending a clinician, practice, or hospital, or asking patients about their confidence in a clinician. The assumption is that patients are likely to recommend—or have confidence in—providers they trust.

As described in Chapter 2, healthcare providers' heroic efforts won short-term gratitude, but winning long-term trust in the face of the changes underway requires more. Applying Frances Frei's model, patients must be confident that their care providers have the following three traits:

1. **Empathy:** Providers grasp what is important to patients.

2. **Authenticity:** Providers are committed to meeting patients' needs. That goal lies at the core of the ego-identities of the organization's leaders, clinicians, and other personnel.

3. **Logic:** Providers know how to get the job done.

Demonstrating all three of these during calmer times is good and noble work, but the challenge is to demonstrate all three during times of uncertainty. Meeting this challenge requires a high-reliability organization, one that can withstand the stress of pandemics, heat waves, and other external events that affect healthcare delivery. High-reliability operating systems collect and analyze data that is relevant to performance and use it to create insights that management can use to orchestrate the organization's response.

Meeting this challenge also requires care providers to switch their focus from discrete services (e.g., visits, tests, procedures, hospitalizations) to care across the episodes that matter to patients. This switch can be made only with more and better information on what patients care about.

Organizations that seek to build patients' trust should recognize that patients are complex and have complex needs. Only by broadening and deepening the ways in which they listen to their patients can doctors understand the people they aim to serve.

Listening Broadly

In the era ahead, we will need to broaden our concept of how to listen to patients. No longer can hospitals or physician practices give short surveys to a small sample of patients to assure themselves that nothing terrible is happening.

Instead, providers must listen everywhere patients are in contact with the healthcare system, including, for example, as they go through pre-visit processes such as scheduling visits or seeking information. Instead, organizations need to engage every time patients do. This aim is ambitious, but nothing less will enable the personalization of care at scale.

Omnichannel listening is where healthcare is heading. It involves combining information from short surveys after specific interactions with more comprehensive traditional surveys after events like visits and hospitalizations. These results can be integrated with those from other tools that assess how people feel about the care they had during a particular episode.

Structured surveys will continue to be valuable for assessing how reliably we provide key drivers of loyalty, and they will likely continue to be conducted via mail, telephone, patient portals, email, and text messages. However, the mix will skew away from telephone and toward digital modes. Some organizations still like to use telephone surveys, in part because that enables them to use the same benchmarks year after year. But the numbers of patients who answer telephone surveys are dwindling, and few of the managers of organizations who use phone surveys answer them themselves.

Digital surveys can now be used to collect data at pain points (e g., scheduling appointments) or when service failures have occurred. While having timely insight into service failures is valuable when making immediate corrections, no organization should make service corrections the major focus of their patient-experience work. While service correction might help an organization that is doing poorly approach average performance measures, on its own it cannot bring an organization into the top quartile of performers.

Listening more broadly does not mean asking only a few questions with shallower answers. However, organizations should avoid overwhelming patients with long surveys. Fortunately, modern survey techniques can help organizations get the data they need to drive improvement without overwhelming their patients.

Listening Deeply

Listening more broadly to patients isn't enough. Organizations need to go deeper, too. High-level global measures that might serve as the focus for the CEO or the board (e.g., Net Promoter Score) give senior leaders insights into how things are going, but they do not provide the data needed to guide efforts to improve. Going deeper means looking beyond survey questions about processes (e.g., did the care providers give follow-up on laboratory tests?) and even beyond more open-ended survey questions (e.g., did the provider show respect?).

As valuable as such survey questions can be, they reveal data only about what they ask. The joke that is relevant to this point describes the inebriated man looking for his lost keys under a streetlight. When asked if this is where he lost them, he says no, but explains that he is looking there because it is the only place where there is enough light to see them.

The implication for healthcare organizations seeking to build trust with patients during times of uncertainty is that they need tools that go beyond those used in the past to understand patients' perspectives. For example, an increasing number of organizations are integrating patient-reported outcome measures (PROMs) into routine care. University of Rochester Medical Center and Henry Ford Health System collect PROMs data from the processes through which their clinicians interact with patients and the electronic medical record.[2]

Artificial intelligence (AI) and natural language processing (NLP)—the branch of AI that enables computers to understand speech the way humans do—can analyze narrative data for deeper information about what matters to patients. For example, a question like "How often did your doctor explain things in a way you could understand?" can provide insight into whether clinicians conveyed information, but not about *how* they made patients feel. NLP makes it possible to identify issues that are important to patients but may not be captured by survey questions alone.

Building Trust Among the Workforce

Frei's model relies in part on logic for building trust among patients; hence, organizations must show that they know what to do to meet their patients' needs and how to do it. This cannot be accomplished without an engaged workforce where the employees have trust in their organizations.

The likelihood that patients would recommend their provider is the best single marker for patients' trust in their caregivers, and the equivalent metric for assessing trust among the healthcare workforce is the likelihood that an employee will stay at their organization. Some employees leave their positions when other jobs offer better opportunities for growth and higher incomes. In other cases, organizations lose desirable employees who take jobs that are essentially no better. This is when organizations should worry. These losses represent evidence that employees did not trust the organization as the best place for their future.

My colleagues performed analyses of the factors that correlate most strongly with employees' likelihood of leaving an organization. Most readers won't be surprised to learn that there are correlations between employees' stated readiness to consider leaving and *many* factors. What might surprise readers is the *strength* of the correlation, and the underlying *details*.

Among 410,000 employers surveyed in 2021, respondents who gave their organizations low scores on valuing diversity were 4.6 times as likely to give unfavorable scores when asked about their intent to stay at the organization. Agreement with the following statements correlated even more strongly with employees' reported likelihood of staying:

- I like the work I do.

- My work is meaningful.

- The work I do makes a real difference.

- I see every patient as an individual patient with specific needs.

- This organization provides high-quality care and service.

- This organization conducts business in an ethical manner.

- This organization treats employees with respect.

- This organization values employees from different backgrounds.

An important subsidiary analysis of these data shows that employees in *every* role in healthcare organizations are most strongly motivated by lofty goals. This analysis shows that employees whose direct contact with patients is limited (e.g., security, clerical, and maintenance personnel) place high value on whether the organization delivers patient-centered care in which every patient is seen as an individual. The organization's commitment to quality is also among the top factors for every nonclinical personnel category. These results demonstrate the need for leaders and managers to show that they share these values, are committed to them, and are focused and effective in pursuing them—no matter how uncertain the times.

The work of building trust in the workforce does not end with commitment to delivering patient-centered care that is safe and high quality. Like patients, employees also have needs and fears, and organizations must apply the same principles that are useful for building trust in patients. For example, in the last few years employees have expressed concern about their own safety and uncertainty about whether they feel they belong at an institution.

Trust-building principles include listening broadly and deeply to employees. They go beyond town-hall–style meetings where, in theory, leaders listen to anyone who speaks up. Building trust takes more than employee engagement surveys performed every year or two. Today, pulse surveying—more frequent and focused surveying—is becoming the norm for understanding what different segments of the workforce are experiencing.

Segmentation is critical. Even though all types of employees share common values, *they need the equivalent of patient-centered care*. There are groups within groups that warrant tailored interventions, as will be discussed in Chapter 9. The ultimate goal is for every individual employee to feel respected and valued for who they are and for the work that they do. If an organization can authentically and effectively help its employees pursue their goals and address their fears, it will have established the basis for trust.

Deepening and Broadening Safety

Like other key elements in healthcare's value chain, the concept of safety has broadened and deepened in multiple ways. Patient safety has been most highly developed as a focus for inpatient care and emergency medicine, but now that focus has broadened to include safety in all settings, including ambulatory care, telemedicine interactions, and nonacute care. This is just a step on the way to thinking about safety according to the units of analysis that matter to patients, episodes that often cut across various settings.

The concept of safety has also deepened to include more than the obvious injuries caused by medical errors. For example, when clinicians make diagnostic errors that could have been avoided, or when diagnoses are delayed by system dysfunction, the organization should acknowledge its missteps, analyze the causes, and take steps to prevent their recurrence.

Safety concerns must also extend to the healthcare workforce. Aside from the risk of infection from Covid-19, the past few years have seen a marked increase in violence and psychological harm toward healthcare personnel by patients and their families. The resultant stress contributed to an increase in burnout and depression among care providers, sometimes culminating in employees leaving their organizations, leaving their professions, or even harming themselves.

Commitment to an enhanced concept of safety is essential to earning the trust of patients and of caregivers. The nature of commitment to this broadened and deepened perspective on safety will be explored in detail in Chapter 8.

Committing to Diversity, Equity, and Inclusion

There was a time when attention to DEI was an extra, something added to agendas for board meetings to show that the organization had a social conscience. Today, DEI is an operational imperative, and in the years ahead it will be an important source of competitive advantage. Organizations must work to improve the diversity of their management teams and their workforces. They must work to improve the equity of their care. And they must work to improve the inclusiveness of their cultures. The organizations that are most effective in doing so will be the most successful in recruiting and retaining the employees they want and in delivering excellent care.

Like other activities in the value chain, the work of pursuing excellence in DEI requires broadening and deepening current programs. It requires pushing for diversity in management as well as at the front lines of care. It takes a long time to increase the number of physicians and other clinicians from underrepresented minorities.

Excellence in DEI requires a system of operating in which data on how patients and employees identify themselves are reliably captured. It also requires surveys of the experiences of both groups to reveal how they regard the equity and inclusiveness of their organization. These data must be captured at precisely defined units of organization (e.g., individual patient-care units) because the cultures at these levels are what matter most to patients and employees on a day-to-day basis. The data must be rich enough to allow segmentation beyond the broad categories defined by race and ethnicity.

The challenges of advancing DEI are considerable, but the rewards are enormous. DEI is essential to earning the trust of patients and the workforce. It is impossible to have a culture of high reliability and safety unless everyone feels enabled to speak up when they see problems that should be addressed.

Responding to Consumerism

In the past, many people working in healthcare (especially physicians) regarded the concepts of consumerism and customers with disdain. These days, few bother to object to these terms because they are too busy responding to the changing healthcare environment where information flows rapidly and people spend more time interacting with the world through the internet. At the 2022 J.P. Morgan Healthcare Conference, leaders of major healthcare systems described strategies to seek competitive differentiation through innovations aimed at potential patients who have choices about where they go for care.

Imagine people you may know who fit this general profile: baby boomers who are internet savvy, who are getting older and are not particularly happy about it, and who want the peace of mind of knowing that they have done their best to optimize their healthcare. They want the best and are willing to travel long distances to get it, even if it means driving past hospitals and medical practices close to home. They are also ready to ask, "Do I really need to come in for this?" when it seems possible to do something without face-to-face contact.

Patients like these are not going to be satisfied by limited, cryptic, often inaccurate information about physicians before they go for visits. They are not going to be happy with relying on telephone interactions to make appointments. They are not going to be willing to put up with long waits. They will find another way to meet their needs.

A growing number of organizations are letting patients book their own appointments online rather than by phone, which often entails waiting on hold and occupying another person's time. Booking visits online should be the default before long, but the real test of whether organizations want to make consumers' choices easier will be if they allow booking via third-party sites and payer directories.

Will disrupting the current processes to make things easier for consumers be a tough sell at a time when doctors, nurses, and other healthcare personnel are burned out and exhausted from the pandemic? Maybe. But accepting consumerism should be seen as an extension of providing patient-centered care. It helps organizations win the trust of patients by assuring them that they are making good choices and making it easier and simpler for them to follow through.

Responding to Healthcare Market Change

For decades now, people in healthcare have used the fee-for-service payment system as an explanation for much of the dysfunction in healthcare and as an excuse for the slow pace of changing it. The times ahead will demand that we deliver more. Although fee-for-service is not disappearing any time soon, an increasing proportion of healthcare is being delivered under other payment models. Because healthcare organizations are likely to be working with multiple payment models for the foreseeable future, organizations must figure out how to overcome the weaknesses that fee-for-service creates. That said, the time to plunge into value-based healthcare has arrived. At the J.P. Morgan Healthcare Conference in January 2022, virtually every major system described an acceleration of their adoption of population management contracts like Medicare Advantage and other relationships with accountable care organizations.

For example, Advocate Aurora Health had been building upon a decade or more of experience with managed-care contracting. At the time, 46 percent of their patients were covered either by capitation or shared-savings contracts, while the other 54 percent were covered by fee-for-service contracts. Advocate Aurora Health's leaders reported good financial performance in the contracts in which they are at risk for total costs of care.

Organizations like Prisma Health, a large nonprofit healthcare system in South Carolina, which did not have a prominent history in managed care, also described strategic plans to move in that direction. Prisma Health reported that they have 320,000 patients in risk contracts now but expect to have a million in such relationships by 2030.

Prisma's leaders described a "risk-capable journey" that began with expense reduction, followed by quality payments, followed by shared savings, followed by shared risk, and ultimately leading to capitation. Rather than avoiding risk in its contracts, Prisma was exploring various forms of risk, such as direct-to-employer relationships, Medicare Advantage, commercial risk, bundled payments, and managed Medicaid. Prisma also had "starting point" populations—its own employees and uninsured patients—where they already bore the responsibility for costs. They anticipated that they would soon pass a tipping point in which 30 to 40 percent of their revenue was tied to something other than the volume of services.

That 30 percent number is an important threshold. It is often attributed to Berkeley economist Stephen Shortell, who commented at a meeting that physicians would not change how they practiced if only a small percentage of their care was not fee-for-service. When asked what it would take for them to change, he offered a guess of 30 percent, based on his field research with some physician practices and his gut sense of human nature. Subsequently, evidence from physician practice data indicated that a major change occurred in the 21 to 30 percent range.[3]

What activities must organizations pursue in response to market change? The University of Maryland Medical System offered one useful model at the J.P. Morgan Healthcare Conference. Over the past several decades, the State of Maryland has gradually moved from volume-based payments to fixed revenue models. Instead of being paid on the basis of service volume, as they once were, hospitals were compensated based on the total costs of care per capita.

University of Maryland Medical System's leaders described five phases for their response to the change in environment:

1. 1970s: When all utilization was funded

2. 1980–2013: Reducing per-case utilization and avoiding readmits/short stays

3. 2014–2018: Reducing avoidable hospital utilization

4. 2019–2023: Accountability for total healthcare spending

5. 2024 and beyond: Transformative care-delivery models

An important takeaway from the presentations at the J.P. Morgan Healthcare Conference, and University of Maryland

Medical System in particular, is that the tide of change seems irresistible. Organizations would be wise to look down the road and expect market pressures to intensify for high-value healthcare—care that meets patients' needs at an affordable cost.

The coming decade will bring other important activities to the value chain for healthcare organizations. For example, there will likely be growing pressures for organizations to do their part in slowing climate change and to reduce their adverse environmental impact. But there are immediate pressures and immediate rewards for building patient and workforce trust, deepening and broadening safety, enhancing DEI, responding to consumerism, and responding to market change.

In the next chapter, I'll examine the implications of the enduring challenges we can expect in the years ahead, and the long-term responses for healthcare leadership and management.

CHAPTER 5

New Approaches to Leadership and Management

LEADERS AND MANAGERS need to adopt new mindsets and develop skills that build resilience. As individuals and management teams, healthcare leaders need to cultivate the ability to question their assumptions of how they should work so they can adapt to new circumstances.

Thinking Again

In times of turmoil, healthcare organizations need more than a performance culture; they need a learning culture. They need the ability to recognize when there is a problem, come up with ideas of how to change, test the ideas, figure out what is working, and then institute a new way of doing things. They need the ability to standardize practices, but they also need the ability to nurture variation.

Adam Grant's 2021 book, *Think Again: The Power of Knowing What You Don't Know*, offers insight into how to create this healthy tension. As Grant points out, leaders need a combination of confidence and humility. They need the humility to concede that their current way of doing things isn't perfect, and the confidence to try new approaches.[1]

Their confidence should be based not on their past accomplishments or what they know, but on their ability to learn, to analyze data, to identify when they have been wrong, and to come up with a new approach that just might be better. Grant points out that the election forecasters who have the best records are the most likely to revisit their predictions.[2] He quotes Jeff Bezos: "People who are right a lot listen a lot, and they change their mind a lot. If you don't change your mind frequently, you're going to be wrong a lot."[3]

Confidence and humility is not the only important combination that supports thinking again; psychological safety and accountability comprise another important pair of attributes. Employees at every level of every organization know their work better than anyone else and can identify when they are having an impact and when their time is being wasted. They sense when problems are brewing; however, they need to feel that they are in a safe environment and can speak up.

But psychological safety alone can breed complacency, as noted by Harvard Business School professor Amy Edmondson. It needs to be combined with accountability. In other words, when the people with power recognize how things could improve, they must feel the responsibility to act. In her extremely popular TEDx talk, she explores how the combination can create a psychologically safe workplace in which learning and improvement thrive.[4]

During the past few years, the imperative to adapt on the fly has led some organizations to change the way they work and how they invest resources. Traditionally, in most organizations, major decisions are made once a year at budget time. Of course, if something is an emergency, the organization should be ready to respond right away. But if a new idea does not need to be implemented right away to avoid disaster, then it is likely to be tabled until the budget season, when it can be weighed against other ways to use the organization's energy and resources.

Conventional management thinking like that has been challenged during the Covid-19 pandemic. Barclay Berdan, the CEO of Texas Health Resources, led his organization through an earlier infectious disease–related crisis in 2015, when they had a patient die from Ebola after being sent home from the emergency department and two nurses became infected. When Covid-19 arrived in 2020, Berdan and his team were ready to respond, and they quickly implemented programs to reassure patients and their employees. But as the pandemic ground on and on, they realized that they needed to, as Berdan put it, "get better at learning and adapting quickly."[5]

Texas Health Resources moved to quarterly planning and modified the budget process to allow frequent adjustments. As Berdan explains, "We have more disciplined and defined system priorities, and we focused on what actionable steps we can implement or achieve in three-month chunks of time. We are seeing little steps add up to big change, and I'm excited about where this approach has taken us."[6]

When managers interact more frequently, they tend to learn faster and work better together. Some organizations, like Mayo Clinic and Mass General Brigham, now use open offices for their senior teams. Meritus Health replaced weekly sit-down meetings that included its dozen senior leaders with daily huddles in the hallway held five times a week and lasting for 15 minutes.

In sum, hardwiring the mindset to think again is a continuous process. It begins with leaders and managers reconsidering how they think about what they know and requires frequent collection and analysis of data and discussing how to proceed in an environment in which everyone feels safe, but responsible for responding.

New Organizational Structures

The need for nimbleness is accelerating the evolution of organizational structures oriented around physician expertise to those oriented around service lines and high-performing, integrated teams that are structured around meeting patients' needs. This trend, underway before the Covid-19 pandemic arrived, was put into a higher gear by the need to redesign care in ways that are not defined by the facilities that have traditionally delivered it.

On the one hand, organizations with multiple hospitals realized during the first phases of the pandemic that they could not let each hospital redesign care for every patient segment on its own. They also realized that their effectiveness in redesigning care was limited when, for example, medical directors who were primary-care physicians were telling specialists what to do. On the other hand, organizations with system-wide specialists leading service lines were able to make plans and implement them.

In the longer-term, even in the absence of pandemic-induced shutdowns, service lines are likely to be critical for addressing the challenges described in Chapter 4. For example, a consistent approach to consumerism can help build trust for all parts of an organization's orthopedics service line, but it requires the entire service line to be consistent in how it interfaces with the outside world. Similarly, an effective service line can enable a delivery system to negotiate bundled payment contracts that could lead to increased market share and also reward providers for greater efficiency and quality.

For analogous reasons, the importance of high-performing multidisciplinary teams organized around patient segments will likely increase in the years ahead. The gold standard of such teams is integrated practice units (IPUs),[7] which include both clinical and nonclinical personnel who work together to provide the full cycle of care for a group of patients, usually defined by a medical condition.

The need for such teams is growing because scientific progress has already shifted the expertise required to manage common conditions beyond the comfort zones of most physicians. For example, a decade ago, I was completely comfortable taking care of patients with diabetes or atrial fibrillation. Today, new medications are available that can help patients with diabetes to lose weight, and invasive procedures can prevent recurrent atrial fibrillation. The sophistication required to choose among cutting-edge interventions means that I have to consult with the diabetes and atrial fibrillation teams at my institution for help with some regularity.

The concept of organizing care around patient segments goes beyond groups defined by conditions. For example, consider how Judd Hollander of Jefferson Health and Rahul Sharma of Weill Cornell Medical College reimagined emergency medicine care. Both are leaders in that field as well as leaders in telemedicine at their organizations.[8] In a 2021 article in *NEJM Catalyst*, they describe the core competency of emergency medicine providers as "being available" to evaluate patients with life-threatening problems for the need for immediate care; they have coined the term *availablist* for their specialty. They construct a framework for segmenting patients who need immediate attention and, even before patients reach the hospital, availablists can begin treatment using tools such as asynchronous text messaging, telephone visits, and audio-video visits to mobile stroke units. The core concept of their work is organizing care around segments of patients according to their needs, not around the bricks-and-mortar of facilities or the expertise of physicians.

Service lines and teams disrupt the status quo, and a natural reflex is to worry that segmentation might not work for all patients, but healthcare organizations should resist becoming paralyzed by identifying exceptions. They should design their structures in ways that optimize care delivery for most patients and make their systems robust enough to detect and care for the exceptions.

New Roles

As healthcare organizations address new challenges, they must let traditional roles evolve and create new ones. For that reason, a range of new titles is showing up on organization charts, and the corresponding responsibilities are directly tied to some of the key activities in the value chain described in Chapter 4. These include chief experience officer, chief wellness officer, chief health equity officer, chief digital officer, chief consumer officer, and chief value officer. Senior leadership roles have also been created at many organizations for the leaders of ambulatory care, who might have been one or two tiers lower on the organization chart in the past.

The chief human resources officer also has a more prominent role than in the past, and, at many organizations, has become a critical member of the CEO's core group of executives. Similarly, at many organizations, the chief medical officers are playing key roles in redesigning care, such as by making decisions about the adoption of artificial intelligence. They often serve as the face of the company for topics of intense public interest.

As organizations remodel themselves to respond to healthcare's challenges, no single organization chart has emerged as ideal. However, it is clear that various areas of responsibility are interdependent, and it is unlikely that any organization can deliver care that is excellent in quality and safety without engaged and aligned employees. For that reason, it is important that the managers view themselves as members of a team, whether they are serving in the new roles or in expanded versions of old ones. As members of a team, they share responsibility for performance across various service lines. More than the creation of new titles, the real developments of interest are the recognition of new types of work, the understanding that various roles are intertwined, and the introduction of new models for working together.

Extending High Reliability to All Aspects of Performance

The term *high reliability* was introduced to most healthcare organizations during the last two decades as part of work to improve patient safety. More recently, the principles of high reliability have proven to be valuable in helping organizations maintain excellence during prolonged crises. The logical implication is that organizations should work to build the principles of high reliability into their cultures for all types of performance during the uncertain times ahead.

There is no pure experiment that randomly assigned institutions to groups that either had or did not have a high-reliability culture, of course. However, when Press Ganey analyzes data from its surveys of patients and employees, the results consistently show that a strong safety culture correlates with all the other types of excellence organizations want, including lower likelihood of employees leaving, more positive ratings for DEI, better patient experience, and every other metric for quality or efficiency available for analysis. In short, there is every reason to believe that successfully making high-reliability principles social norms within an organization will lead to a wide range of benefits.

It now appears that one of those benefits is the ability to manage crises. Houston Methodist provides a good real-world example of what it means to make a commitment to high reliability, and the benefits of doing so during times of duress. As key leaders including their CEO, Marc L. Boom, have described, "Our focus for the past decade has been to become an HRO [high-reliability organization] and a learning healthcare system where we can safely perform our normal work on a daily basis and seamlessly shift into disaster mode, when necessary, without sacrificing the quality of care for our patients or the well-being of our employees,"[9]

Houston Methodist describes commitment to five principles of high reliability as foundational for their culture:

1. **Deference to expertise:** In healthcare, this means leaders should listen to frontline workers, who *really* know about an organization's operations, and to patients, who are the experts on whether their needs are being met.

2. **Sensitivity to operations:** Healthcare is complex, and so are its operations. Employees working on the front lines are the people most sensitive to flaws in the system and are thus critical to making improvements.

3. **Preoccupation with preventing failure:** High-reliability organizations hate failures, so they work hard to detect them, learn from them, and develop approaches to prevent them.

4. **Reluctance to simplify:** High-reliability organizations don't look for simple answers to complex problems. Instead, they accept that complex systems have multiple areas for potential failure and seek to understand new and unexpected failures.

5. **Promotion of resilience:** High-reliability organizations have the structure, resources, and culture in place to respond to major challenges.

Houston Methodist described extensive work on the development of a culture of safety and the infrastructure for a learning healthcare system. This infrastructure includes measurement systems and expertise with improvement methods such as root-cause analysis and Lean Six Sigma.

The payoff of this work has been improvement in quality measures. For example, sepsis-associated deaths fell from 35 percent of inpatient deaths in 2008 to 8.2 percent in 2022. Houston Methodist has high rankings in national report cards on quality and safety. Surveys of employee engagement have yielded top-decile performance on survey items directly related to high-reliability culture, such as "Mistakes have led to positive change here" and "When a mistake is reported, it feels like the focus is on solving the problem, not writing up the person."

When the Covid-19 pandemic hit, Houston Methodist applied all five of its principles of high reliability when designing their response. Its leaders feel strongly that the organization's history of incorporating these principles in their operations over the course of several years made them resilient and better able to adapt to the unexpected.

Implementing a Data Strategy

Good intentions and inspirational speeches are no substitute for an operating system to support excellence in high reliability. Leadership needs a balanced scorecard that captures progress on the activities described in Chapter 4 and which is supported by an effective data strategy. Moreover, as noted in the preceding sections, the entire management team should own responsibility for progress.

The realization that healthcare has a serious data problem has driven the need for data strategy in healthcare organizations. Industry leaders are both addicted to and overwhelmed by the flood of data. It flows in 24/7 through multiple portals, and organizations spend millions getting the data into reports that often go unused. Faced with an onslaught of red, yellow, and green boxes, managers can't be blamed for saying, "Just tell me what to do."

The search for simplicity can take organizations to dangerous places. Leaders at the top often look for one or two measures that summarize everything—and those measures do not serve as concrete guides for managers in need of improvement. In the absence of effective guidance, leaders choose priorities based on anecdotes and their instincts. Managers view the complex work of management as a series of siloed initiatives.

What healthcare leaders and managers need instead is an enterprise-wide data strategy that manages complexity and makes it simple for the user. Such strategies recognize that there are many customers for data in an organization, but no one needs to see it all. The CEO needs one view of the data, and the frontline manager needs a different view. Organizations need an overall plan to get managers the right data with the right analyses at the right time for them to translate information into action.

Data collection is just the first step of the hard work in understanding what is signal and what is noise. Then comes the even harder work of translating analyses into insights. The final step is using those insights to develop priorities for management and improvement. This sequence should not be performed just once for an organization; it must be performed for all the units of analysis at which management occurs.

Currently, at many organizations, operational data are routinely fed through enterprise data warehouses to operating command centers for analysis and report preparation. Managers receive updates, often from multiple sources, about performance in their own local areas of control—quality, safety, patient experience, volume, financial performance, and so on. Information flows so readily that every patient has become a big data challenge for clinicians, and every unit of organization has become a big data challenge for managers.

Some organizations have responded to what is widely known as analysis paralysis by adopting tactics from consumerism, emphasizing more frequent collection of fewer data points (e.g., using smartphone apps to survey patients at several points during a healthcare episode to detect problems). This tactic is useful for *service recovery* (i.e., apologizing when things have gone wrong), but that cannot be the only tactic used if organizations want to reach the top tiers of performance ratings.

As noted earlier, many organizations are changing how they are structured, and thus how data are collected, analyzed, and reported. Such changes reflect the insight that the needs of patients define the nature of performance, and that personalized care can be best delivered by organizing it around groups of patients who are typically defined by their diagnoses. Therefore, service lines, institutes, and centers (e.g., cardiac, orthopedic, cancer) are increasingly important units of organization and data reporting.

My colleague Deirdre Mylod and I outlined the key steps in developing an organizational data strategy:[10]

1. **Segment the customers for data:** For example, boards and CEOs need summary information about outcome measures across all domains of quality aggregated up to the full entity. Senior leaders need more granular information that connects high-level outcomes with the key leading indicators that will influence those outcomes. Frontline managers and staff need frequent data related to all aspects of operations critical to performance.

2. **Create value through data:** No one should receive a data dump. Instead, delivered data should enable users to create value for the organization through these key activities:

a. Selecting key performance indicators

b. Knowing current performance status

c. Tracking trends

d. Identifying priorities

e. Investigating variation in performance

f. Setting goals

3. **Deepen value through data integration:**

   a. Integrate the data on a domain for quality (e.g., safety or patient experience) within one setting.

   b. Integrate data on a domain for quality across settings.

   c. Integrate data across all domains of quality for the overall population.

4. **Deepen value through integrated analytics:** Because various dimensions of performance are intertwined and all tied to having an engaged workforce, the data should be seen not as a reflection of siloed initiatives, but instead as a reflection of a holistic concept of excellence.

5. **Establish priorities for managers at key units of analysis (e.g., service lines):** Doing so streamlines data by focusing on the most important drivers of performance.

6. **Deliver customer-specific information:** Choose a format that is most helpful to the user. For example, board members tend to prefer report cards highlighting strengths and weaknesses, while senior managers might want trend lines that indicate improvement or deterioration.

Putting this full-blown data strategy in place represents a significant investment of time and resources, but the alternatives—being overwhelmed by data that does not get used or having too little data for managers to effect improvement—won't enable healthcare organizations to learn, adapt, and improve.

This concludes Part II of this book. Part III will turn to each component of the value chain of activities described in Chapter 4 and explore how to achieve excellence in them.

EXCELLENCE IN THE FUTURE: GOING DEEPER AND BROADER

CHAPTER SIX

Earning the Trust of Patients

THE FUNDAMENTALS STILL apply when it comes to earning the trust of patients, but to retain and build that trust requires broadening and deepening our understanding of patients' needs. In this context, broadening means extending our understanding to the entire set of interactions that matter to patients, including going beyond the one-to-one clinician-patient relationship and building trust with patients' families and the community. Deepening means going far beyond the topics captured in standard measures to get at more subtle issues that inspire confidence or concern, like the good and bad ways caregivers use humor in their interactions with patients.

The standards are higher now. Patients want their care to be cutting edge. They also know that their care is a team activity, and they will directly ask, "Have you talked to Dr. So-and-so?" They want their care to be coordinated, and they have become sophisticated enough to worry about issues like "Who will actually be doing my procedure?" and "Will you be doing more than one operation at the same time?" They are increasingly aware of the nature of delivery systems. I have had patients ask, "Are you *really* a system?" and draw comfort from my reassurances about the flow of information and ability to get care at many locations.

But people know talk is cheap. Every instance in which communication is poor and care is uncoordinated rattles patients' trust. Trust erodes when patients see that different parts of the healthcare system are not in sync. For example, when they learn at the pharmacy that medications prescribed by their doctor are not covered by their health plan, they may wonder, "What else can't they get right?"

In one-to-one, in-person interactions with patients, clinicians must deliver compassionate, coordinated care. But organizations must also build trust before, after, and in-between those in-person contacts. They should look for chaos and friction, and work to reduce them. They should go beyond cultivating empathy in individual clinicians to hardwiring critical values in teams. And they must work with insurers, government agencies, and even competitors across the value chain of activities that affect patients' care.

The Basics

Excellence at the level of the individual caregiver has not gone out of style; patients still treasure interactions in which clinicians treat them with compassion and respect. In the future, patients may have high-frequency, low-stakes interactions with robots or bots— software programs that can perform automated tasks like answering frequently asked questions. But when the stakes are high, human interaction is essential. When they have a serious illness or develop frightening symptoms, patients will always need to be cared for by clinicians with empathy, kindness, attentiveness, and attention to coordination.

Cultivating these characteristics among caregivers is both difficult and gratifying. It demands the application of high-reliability principles to patient-centeredness. It doesn't require caregivers to become better people, but it *does* require social norms in which caregivers are at their best with every patient.

It also requires creating social capital by standardizing the way caregivers work with each other and how they interact with patients. For example, nursing leaders now cite the "Nursing Bundle" of best practices that should be used 100 percent of the time: hourly purposeful rounding, leader rounding, and bedside shift reports. These leaders emphasize not just *what* should happen, but *how* it should happen, moving away from task orientation and prioritizing human connection.

When performed effectively, this process provides a structured means of promoting communication between patients, families, and employees. It has been shown to reduce complications and improve patient experience. The same beneficial effects can be produced by other structured processes aimed at improving teamwork and communication in other contexts, such as huddles in ambulatory settings.

But the trust of patients cannot be earned simply by having management impose these processes upon caregivers. Hourly rounding doesn't work if staff just stick their heads in the door and then check off a box. Huddles don't work if caregivers don't use the opportunity to raise issues, solve problems, and stay focused on common goals.

Ritualizing these basic functions can help achieve high reliability. Many experts like the idea of habits, but, perhaps because I am the child of Chinese immigrants, I like the idea of rituals as a way of earning the trust of patients. To explain why, I'll delve a bit into the teachings of someone whose name doesn't come up much in books on healthcare quality—Confucius, the Chinese philosopher who lived from 551 to 479 BCE.

Simply put, Confucius believed that life is complicated, and that it is often hard to know the right thing to do. Happily, however, rituals provide frequent predictable moments in which we can behave as if we are actualizing our best selves. An older person enters the room, and we stand up, as if we were respectful. Someone gives us a gift, and we say thank you, as if we were grateful. By behaving *as if* we are the way we should be at these moments, we hone our instincts and respond better in moments when the right thing to do may not be apparent.

Applying this philosophy to patient care is not a stretch. For example, consider the ritual of finding a chair to sit at the same level as a patient in a bed as if one weren't in a hurry to get on to the next patient, and as if one didn't want the patient to feel an imbalance of power. A study of 120 patients recovering from elective spine surgery validated the value of this simple act. The patients were randomly assigned to two groups, one in which the clinicians sat down and the other in which they remained standing. Patients perceived the clinicians who sat down as spending a longer time at their bedside, even though the actual times were the same. They also reported a more positive interaction with the clinicians who sat, and believed that they imparted a better understanding of their condition.[1] Even in the absence of such data, Confucius would likely have believed that this particular ritual helps build trust in patients, and also helps clinicians be at their best in the discussions that follow.

The relationship between rituals and trust was demonstrated when Atul Gawande, one of my colleagues at Brigham and Women's Hospital, was advancing the idea of a surgical safety checklist. He and his colleagues showed that a 19-item checklist designed to improve team communication and consistency of care reduced complication rates, but many surgeons—including those at our own hospital—resisted the idea. For example, they thought that pausing to have all team members introduce themselves by name and role was a waste of time and discounted the argument that the introductions might lower individuals' threshold for speaking up if something seemed not quite right.

Nevertheless, surveys found that more than 90 percent of surgeons, nurses, and other caregivers would want the checklist used if they or a close family member were undergoing surgery.[2] Even in a skeptical crowd, this ritual inspired trust. The data helped convince operating room staffs around the world to make the checklist a norm.

Such rituals help inspire trust if they are performed with the knowledge of patients, either with them or in their presence. These types of transparency make it clear to patients and families that the basics are indeed covered. Hourly rounding, for example, is valuable because it enables frequent assessment of patients' needs, but it also assures patients that they have not been forgotten, and that their caregivers are attentive. In short, transparency conveys authenticity—and thus inspires trust.

One of my favorite examples of employing transparency to inspire trust is a practice that has evolved at several emergency departments with excellent patient-experience performance. Independently, staff at several emergency departments have developed a standardized process in which the last person to see a patient before the physician comes in mentions the physician by name (e.g., "You'll be seeing Dr. Smith"). If they can add something, anything about the physician, they do (e.g., "our kids go to the same school"). The implied message is "We are part of a team, and we know and like each other."

Sharing the information that caregivers are functioning like a team helps build patients' trust. For this reason, I do all I can to ensure that my patients know that my colleagues and I are working together. I start visits by telling patients I have read the notes from the other clinicians or have seen the information from other provider organizations. I let them know that I will be in touch with their other caregivers and tell them when those conversations have occurred.

The best way to demonstrate teamwork is to be face to face, together with the patient. That is why family meetings with multiple clinicians over Zoom are usually worth the effort to arrange.

Going Broader

Listening to people and conveying that you grasp what matters to them is crucial in building trust. That listening process today should begin well before patients and their families meet with doctors, and it should continue afterward. It also must be done reliably, quickly, conveniently, and in the moment, when friction could occur and improvement is possible.

This broadened notion of the episode reflects the understanding that interactions between clinicians and patients are hugely important determinants of patients' trust, but they are not the only determinants. Chaos, confusion, and delays undermine patients' confidence and trust in their personal healthcare system, and they understand that their doctor is only one part of that system. If patients get incorrect information from websites or cannot reach practices to make appointments or ask questions, they lose confidence in their caregiving system. Then they are likely to remember that they are in fact consumers—people with choices—and they may choose to seek their care elsewhere.

These changes imply the need for fundamental change in thinking about the patient experience. The focus should be redirected from the performance of the clinicians or the organization to what is relevant to the patient. The critical question has shifted from "How did the doctor/nurse do?" to "How is it going for the patient?"

"How is it going?" The question is simple and obvious, but the methods to address it are evolving. Getting the answer takes more than asking patients how things went after a visit or a hospitalization. And it takes more than short surveys at micro-moments, such as when people are booking appointments or paying for their care. In fact, to answer the question "How is it going?" requires collecting data under both types of circumstances, and the ability to integrate the information to capture the little picture and big picture of each patient's story.

Fortunately, new technology combined with widespread access to smartphones is making it possible to collect and integrate much more data, allowing sophisticated assessments of where opportunities for improvement exist. This type of omnichannel listening requires deeper surveys after patients have had major interactions with healthcare and shorter surveys just as smaller interactions have occurred—an approach that is increasingly familiar to people as they shop, stay in hotels, go through airports, and so on.

The essential technology and expertise to support this data collection come from outside of healthcare, from the customer experience and market research sector, including Forsta, a leader in this area acquired by Press Ganey in 2022. I've been learning a lot as my colleagues and I consider how to combine what Forsta does with traditional surveys.

Not everyone responds to opportunities to give feedback. I know that from personal experience. When my own interactions have gone just fine, I tend to simply delete the text messages asking for feedback. But when there have been problems, I am more likely to let the organization know. And because the goal is perpetual improvement, insights into what isn't going well are valuable.

Such data can help smooth out pre-visit friction and even address problems as they arise.

Some organizations have opted to use consumer-oriented approaches as replacements for traditional measurement and analysis of patient experience. A more strategic approach is to create a synthesis of the real-time data that focus on the most critical value of a transactional interaction (ease, convenience, task completion) and deeper analyses of surveys with greater detail for high-stakes interactions (e.g., the survey after a hospitalization or patient visit) that lend themselves to benchmarking. The two types of measurement are analogous to the two types of thinking Daniel Kahneman describes in *Thinking, Fast and Slow*. They complement each other.

Going broader also means listening to people in other units of analysis (i.e., groups that matter). For this reason, many organizations are now using tools developed for consumer research to conduct virtual focus groups quickly and efficiently. A related tactic is crowd-sourcing, in which groups of people (e.g., employees of the organization or large groups of consumers/patients) can generate ideas for improvement and prioritize them.

None of these tools is state of the science for listening to patients on their own. Collectively, though, these tools can help healthcare organizations understand what people are going through. An additional benefit is that they can *show* people that the organization wants to understand and is working hard to do so.

Going Deeper

Gathering information at friction points over a broader period of time and broader units of analysis should be complemented by going deeper and exploring issues that may not be captured by conventional surveys. One of the most exciting approaches is the use of artificial intelligence (AI) and natural language processing (NLP) to extract insights from narrative data, such as patient comments on surveys.

You don't need to be a psychologist to know that stories are more emotionally engaging than numbers. Like every other physician, I have been obsessed with the content of negative comments from patients. (And I have drawn little solace from positive comments and reassuring quantitative data on the quality of my interactions with patients.) The truth is that you need both stories and data. The data keep you from overreacting to the last story you heard. The stories make it more likely that you react at all. This is why, years ago, I began quoting Amy Compton-Phillips, who, at the time, was the chief clinical officer of Providence Health, when I heard her say that her rule is "No stories without data, no data without stories."[3]

The use of AI and NLP makes it possible to translate stories into data, extract new types of insights that might be missed by survey questions, and retain the emotional engagement that comments generate. Until recently, the unstructured nature of responses to open-ended questions made it difficult to analyze patients' comments for trends and insights. But now technology can harness comments as rich sources of qualitative information that enhance our understanding of individuals' experiences and perceptions, and lend themselves to quantitative analyses in which they are rigorously analyzed en masse.

There are three key steps for harvesting insights from comments. The first is sentiment analysis—the classification of insights as positive, negative, or neutral. It takes AI with deep linguistics expertise to detect the difference between positive and negative sentiment, which can change with just a slight change in wording or syntax. An example is detecting positive sentiment in the comment, "The doctors were kind, I would go back" as opposed to the negative sentiment in the comment, "Were the doctors kind, I would go back." Another example is the difference between "The doctor was cool" and "The doctor was cold."

The second step is theme categorization, the use of NLP to categorize insights into themes and subthemes. Survey data might reveal that patients have reservations about the cleanliness of a facility. The review of comments from dozens or hundreds of patients might reveal *why* ratings of cleanliness are poor. It might be due to untidy bathrooms, soiled linens that are not changed promptly, or staff wearing scrubs with blood stains. Theme categorization can also reveal, for example, that courtesy and respect is the most prominent category for positive insights in many settings of care, while themes for negative insights are highly variable.

The third step is machine learning, in which algorithms are constantly tweaked and trained by humans to fine-tune the sentiment analysis and categorize new sets of comments. Like humans, no two AI/NLP programs are alike. Those that are truly constantly improving will be different a year from now because they are learning.

In 2021 my colleague Senem Guney and I wrote an article in *Harvard Business Review* to illustrate how AI/NLP can provide guidance on subtleties that help make care truly excellent, such as the analysis of the use of humor in patient interactions.[4] To our knowledge, there are *no* survey questions in which patients are asked if they found their doctors or nurses humorous. Our interest in this topic emerged unexpectedly during explorations of a large dataset of patient comments aimed at understanding what patients value most in their care.

We used AI/NLP to extract insights from comments in 988,161 (17 percent inpatient, 83 percent outpatient) surveys of patient experience across the United States during 2020. From these comments, we extracted positive and negative insights, and categorized them into themes and subthemes. We couldn't help but notice that, in these analyses, humor came up repeatedly when patients described experiences with their clinicians (see Tables 6.1 and 6.2).

Table 6.1 How Humor Can Convey Caring

Qualities Humor Can Help Convey	Comments from Patients About Their Experience
Empathy and Compassion	*. . . the nurse who took care of me was amazing . . . very caring and answered all my questions . . . had sense of humor and I liked that.*
Kindness	*Every nurse treated me like a close friend, responding to me extremely fast, and even stayed to converse with me, making me laugh every day.*
Helpfulness	*I had an excellent anesthesiologist who came and explained the procedure, made me laugh, and put me at ease.*
Attentiveness	*[Dr. X] was as always meticulous and competent with his treatments, while being thorough with easy-to-understand explanations of my condition, options, his recommendations, future options, etc, all delivered kindly and with a good sense of both humor and compassion!*
Patience	*[Dr. Y] always provides full explanations well beyond the norm, i.e., anatomical lessons on probable causes of injury (in an interesting and even humorous manner), and answers all patient questions thoroughly without any sense of being rushed or time-pressured.*
Pleasantness	*This provider had a very good bedside manner. He made me laugh many times when I was initially nervous about the appointment.*
Emotional Supportiveness	*[Dr. Z]'s nurse assistant is fabulous. She listens to my medical concerns, is extremely professional, and still has a sense of humor and sensitivity.*

Table 6.2 How Humor Can Convey Lack of Caring

Quality Lacking When Humor Is Inappropriate	Comments from Patients About Their Experience
Empathy and Compassion	*The doctor was the only one to show no respect and even joke at a question I was concerned about.*
Kindness	*When I arrived at triage my water had broken about six hours earlier. I was told that my doctor would likely start me on Pitocin. I let the nurse know that I did not want Pitocin and she made a sarcastic comment along the lines of "we'll see."*
Helpfulness	*My mother drove 1.5 hours to [town] only for [Dr. Q] to question why she was in the rehab hospital for so long, who her doctors were and asked, "What do you want from me?" My mother wanted to get up and leave. He even made a comment "Well I see your CAT scan. Looks like you still have a brain. I see you still have a crack on the skull. Maybe that's why you still have headaches." My mother returned home without any clarity to the cause of her headaches, let alone relief.*
Attentiveness	*The discharge doctor did NOT listen to me or ask me any questions. He tried to be funny, but he was not. A hospital discharge should be taken seriously.*
Patience	*In the recovery room, the nurses were making fun of a patient out loud.*
Pleasantness	*I am Hispanic. I felt as if I was stereotyped. When I asked about carpal tunnel problems that I am having, the doctor told me to try laying off the burritos. Doctor was very arrogant.*
Emotional Supportiveness	*Nurses were telling jokes and funny stories with continuous loud laughing. They continued with this [behavior] for one or two hours.*

Our analyses indicate that humor is not the main course when it comes to caring; it is more like a condiment. The *actual* main course that patients appreciate relates to courtesy and respect. Patients don't comment very often on the technical skill of clinicians, but their comments suggest deep appreciation for empathy, kindness, helpfulness, and patience. And when patients note that care with these attributes was accompanied by humor, the humor seems more than welcome.

However, when patients feel the absence of courtesy and respect, the use of humor by caregivers adds insult to injury. One might read the comments in Table 6.2 and feel incredulous that such incidents occurred, but everyone in healthcare has probably witnessed colleagues making jokes to amuse their colleagues or themselves.

The use of AI/NLP shows that humor is not a stand-alone asset or liability. It serves to amplify the positive or the negative signals that patients pick up from their doctors and nurses. Humor offered for no purpose other than providing a distraction is irritating. Humor in the absence of obvious courtesy and respect can be taken as callous disregard. But when humor is a subsidiary component of meaningful interactions between clinicians and patients, it can break down the line that separates them.

That Period Before Diagnoses Are Made

Healthcare providers have worked hard to improve efficiency—especially the speed and quality of care for patients after a diagnosis—but there is a wide-open opportunity for building trust in that anxiety-filled period beforehand. It begins when patients realize that they have a new, unexplained symptom and they think, "What the heck?" The anxiety usually continues until there is a diagnosis and a plan that they believe in.

This period is essentially unmeasured and therefore unmanaged in most healthcare settings. Thus, it is fraught with long delays, dropped balls, and bumbled communications with worried patients and families. In short, it is a period full of psychological suffering, during which patients wonder if their caregivers understand their concerns. It is therefore part of the episode of care that offers the opportunity to build trust.

Dana-Farber Brigham Cancer Center strives to minimize psychological suffering through their Cancer Diagnostic Service—a team that expedites diagnosis for patients who present with signs or symptoms of cancer, and where the appropriate next steps are unclear. The frontline physicians are internists, rather than oncologists. They see patients right away, thoroughly review records, and conduct comprehensive diagnostic workups with input from consulting oncologists.

Here is an example from my own primary care practice. This story began on a Monday morning in the fall of 2021, when one of my patients called me to say she had woken up and felt a hard lump on her neck. I called the cancer center, and the internist, Louise Schneider, said she would see the patient the next morning at 10. Schneider went ahead and, even before she or I had seen the patient, booked a CT scan with contrast for early on Tuesday afternoon and a biopsy for Wednesday. By Friday, the pathology report was back. The patient had a lymphoma that lent itself to chemotherapy. My patient and her daughter met with an oncologist who specializes in lymphoma on Friday afternoon to plan her treatment, which started the next Monday.

Another care delivery model that helps build trust is exemplified by a breast cancer screening program developed in 2007 by a young radiologist, Emily Sedgwick, at Baylor College of Medicine. Aiming to minimize fear, she created a program to offer core needle biopsies on the same day a worrisome finding is detected. Designing care to minimize anguish took commitment and management, but efforts led to eightfold growth in the program, reflecting patients' trust that the caregivers understood their fears.

Beyond the Clinician-Patient Relationship

The relationships between patients and their individual caregivers will always matter, of course, but healthcare excellence today also requires building trust at two additional levels. The first occurs between the care team and the patient's family, and the second between the healthcare system and its community.

Medicine is so complex today that sophisticated care virtually always involves a team of clinicians. Many families are also closely connected, and they often use smartphones and internet apps to stay in touch. The reality is that healthcare interactions go beyond the doctor-patient relationship and constitute something more like a social network. The ability for families and healthcare teams to connect immediately across long distances has changed expectations for how healthcare professionals communicate with those in their care. The risks for disappointment are rife, as are the opportunities for building trust.

I'm thinking now (and wincing as I do) of the Zoom family meeting I recently had with a 92-year-old patient and his son and daughter after he had a series of emergency department visits for lightheadedness. The son started off with angry accusations about the quality of care; he had not been part of my discussions with the patient and his sister. After about 10 minutes, he calmed down— in part because of information that I shared with him, but also because of feedback from the other members of his family.

Although the outcome in this case was good (thanks in large part to technology), the takeaway message is that, to effectively treat an increasingly elderly population with an array of chronic diseases, real trust requires not only expertise by clinicians, but also coordination and communication with the patient's family. Thus, the relationship between the care team and the patient's family can be expected to emerge as a new focus in the pursuit of excellence.

Of course, families are highly variable, and many patients don't have *any* supportive relatives ready to step forward. Confidentiality issues are complicating factors, too. But these concerns should not stand in the way of developing approaches that support trusting relationships between family members and care teams when everyone is working together for the patient's best interests. Those wonderful collaborations should not seem like they occurred by accident. Instead, practices like Zoom family meetings should be routine in clinical contexts like intensive care or oncology, where trust is most critical.

The importance of the relationship between the delivery system and the community became apparent in the very early days of the Covid-19 pandemic. In March 2020, physicians working at the Papa Giovanni XXIII Hospital in Bergamo, a beautiful ancient city in the Lombardy region of Italy, described how their brand-new, state-of-the-art facility with 48 intensive care beds was being overwhelmed and becoming a site of transmission. At one point that month, they had 4,305 cases.[5]

The report they wrote for *NEJM Catalyst* was the most widely read article of the year for the publication. The crisis in Bergamo forced these physicians to see that what they were doing was not enough. "Pandemic solutions are required for the entire population, not only for hospitals," they wrote, calling to move healthcare for everyone but the most critically ill from the hospitals and into the community.

Of course, patient-centered care should not be discarded. But for people to have trust in their healthcare, clinicians must be part of systems that are working with the rest of society to address larger needs.

Transparency as a Trust-Building Tactic

As noted earlier in this chapter, when discussing the basics of interactions with patients, transparency is an invaluable tool for building trust. Recall Frances Frei's three components for building trust: empathy, authenticity, and logic. Transparency can convey empathy, it is essential to authenticity, and it can convince patients of the effectiveness of the organization's logic.

I am well aware of the ambivalence many of my colleagues in healthcare have when they hear the word *transparency*. The concern is that the complexity of our work will not be considered if we disclose our imperfections. Nevertheless, everyone wants transparency from those around them, so it is a reasonable expectation that patients and their families want transparency from healthcare organizations—and are likely to withhold their trust if they suspect that transparency is lacking.

My recommendation is that leaders of healthcare organizations commit to transparency and push it as far as possible. The basic operating principle should be to share everything unless a compelling reason can be offered that the harm will exceed the benefits.

My colleagues and I have pushed for transparency in posting patient comments about physicians, which is still not a norm in healthcare, but it's getting close. It's clear that patients really value them, and the absence of comments online doesn't help build trust in the physician or the organization.

In fact, the strategic step for healthcare organizations is to go beyond sharing patients' comments about physicians on the organization's website and export these data to third-party sites like

Healthgrades and payer directories, so that patients/consumers see the same robust information across multiple sites. When they see that consistency, their trust goes up. No one feels great about choosing something that rates five stars on one or two sites, but two or three stars on others.

The ideal goal is to build a culture of transparency, with four interrelated domains described in a white paper, entitled *Shining a Light*, from the IHI Lucian Leape Institute.[6] These four domains are:

1. Between clinicians and patients (e.g., transparency with patient comments)

2. Among clinicians (e.g., unblinded sharing of data on quality and efficiency)

3. Among organizations (e.g., unblinded sharing of performance data)

4. With the public (e.g., public reporting of safety data)

All four types of transparency are demanding—indeed, sometimes excruciating. The temptation for leaders who view disquieting information is to wonder whether it really should be shared. When the goal of building trust with patients is kept in mind, the answer is almost always yes.

High Reliability and the Anna Karenina Principle

Listening to patients and families and being authentic in sharing their values is not the entire story. As Frances Frei's model makes clear, organizations must be effective in pursuing those values to build trust. That means thinking clearly about what should be done and sharing the results so that patients (and employees) know that they are good hands.

Patients trust their caregivers when they know their caregivers adhere to high-reliability principles. Caregivers who are trusted don't turn these principles on when they want to; they are at their best in every interaction. These caregivers despise failure, so much so that they acknowledge it when it occurs and try to learn how to prevent it. Caregivers who are trusted take these high-reliability principles, which are developed as part of the safety movement, and extend them to other dimensions of quality, including patient experience.

For the purpose of inspiring trust, there are *two* types of high reliability, which Senem Guney and I described in a *Harvard Business Review* article as being consistent with the Anna Karenina principle.[7] That principle is an adaption of the famous first line from Tolstoy's novel *Anna Karenina*: "Happy families are all alike; every unhappy family is unhappy in its own way." Extending this principle to healthcare means that we should always do the small number of things that are essential for building patients' trust, and we must constantly work to prevent the many, many things that might erode trust.

Support for the Anna Karenina principle comes from our analyses of millions of comments from many institutions, which have consistently found that courtesy and respect dominate positive insights in virtually every setting of care. In fact, we have yet to find an institution or unit of patient care in which courtesy and respect are not the most important positive themes. The major subthemes of courtesy and respect are shown in Table 6.1, and include empathy, kindness, attentiveness, patience, and compassion. These are the features of care that are *always* present in the healthcare equivalent of Tolstoy's happy families.

The consistency in positive insights is strikingly different from the variation among the negative comments—the characteristics of care that cause the equivalent of Tolstoy's unhappy families. For example, in one analysis at a major teaching hospital, the themes from negative comments varied markedly across the surgical units, each of which had a different major problem area. For some units, the most frequently noted source of unhappiness was the long wait for assistance. In others, the most common issue was noise. In still others, patients complained about chaos of the discharge process.

These data demonstrate that the challenge of preventing negative experiences requires the same kind of vigilance required in patient safety, where there are so many ways in which care can go wrong, ranging from pressure ulcers to falls to medication errors. One specific issue may emerge as the most common problem on one patient care unit, while another issue is likely to emerge on another unit—and a week later, the problems might be reversed. A bad experience—a patient feeling vulnerable to catching Covid-19 because the bathrooms are not clean—can ruin a good experience created through technically excellent and empathic care.

The nature of these challenges calls for complementary approaches to data collection and analysis. Structured questions in which patients are asked to rate their experiences on Likert-type scales (1–5 scales, with 5 being extremely positive and 1 extremely negative) are efficient for assessing whether positive themes occur reliably. Simply put, the best way to determine if patients were treated with courtesy and respect is asking them directly.

But AI/NLP analysis of narrative data can capture insights and nuances that go beyond the information available from survey questions by extracting insights from thousands of comments— and is thus particularly valuable for understanding what makes unhappy patients unhappy. While patients' checkbox answers to survey questions can identify cleanliness as a problem on a patient care unit, comments can pinpoint specific issues like soiled gowns, litter, or staff failing to sanitize their hands.

These two types of data collection and analysis support caregivers in their dual efforts to earn patients' trust. Clinicians cannot always provide cures or complete relief of suffering, but they *can* be reliable on themes such as courtesy, respect, empathy, coordination, and communication. Ensuring that these positive themes characterize every patient's care requires the establishment and reinforcement of social norms for caregivers.

That work begins at the top for every organization (i.e., leaders must show how important these values are to them), and managers must ensure that these elements are standards of care, not mere guidelines or recommendations. At many organizations, events in which patients are not treated with dignity are reviewed in the same daily meetings as safety events and near-misses.

This form of high reliability should be complemented by systematic efforts to *prevent* recurrences of the wide range of lapses that can be unsettling to patients. When a patient is given contradictory information from different caregivers (one says they are going home tomorrow, and another says they are going to a rehabilitation facility), that is not something to be shrugged off. An error has occurred. It may be no particular individual's fault, and it may not have caused physical harm to a patient. But it is a system failure, and one that understandably shakes patients' confidence in their care. These types of events should be detected and analyzed, and the response should be akin to the error-trapping approaches developed in patient safety programs.

The work of preventing the many possible causes of failure from the perspective of patients is enormous and can be consuming. But the work of preventing failures should not distract healthcare organizations from ensuring the reliability of positive themes. To make care excellent, we must be highly reliable in developing cultural norms and preventing failures so that every patient can be like a member of Tolstoy's happy families.

Building trust in this way among patients is not possible without building trust among the people who are delivering their care. And that will be the topic that we turn to next, using some of the same approaches that we have just considered for patients and their families.

CHAPTER 7

Earning the Trust of the Workforce

WORKFORCE WELL-BEING IS the crisis of the moment, and it looks like this moment is going to last a long time, well beyond the end of the Covid-19 pandemic. Every healthcare organization is having difficulty hiring and retaining employees of all types—clinical and nonclinical. Every organization has increased its compensation spending, and also discovered that money is only part of the answer to their human resources challenges. Some organizations are working to cultivate the long-term pipeline, but increasing numbers of employees is not likely to be the full solution either.

Organizations first need to attract good clinicians and other types of employees, then they need to retain them. To accomplish that that during times of uncertainty, healthcare organizations need to build the trust of their workforces. They want employees who might consider jobs elsewhere to want to stay with colleagues they know and trust.

Trust is also important because healthcare organizations need their employees to have multiple forms of resilience when crises arise. One type of resilience is the ability to recover from the intense stresses of their work. Another is the ability and willingness to adapt to new challenges. A third is a group characteristic, the ability of team members to change how they work together to meet the needs of the moment. Those team members need to be able to trust each other and know that their close colleagues will rise to the occasion, too, no matter what situation they might face.

All three types of resilience are essential to organizations' ability to inspire trust in patients, and all three depend on the ability of the organizations to cultivate trust among their employees. That ability depends on organizations demonstrating the key elements of Frances Frei's model for trust—empathy, authenticity, and logic—to their staffs.

The targets for trust cultivation go beyond nurses and doctors. As every manager in healthcare learned during Covid-19, *all* types of personnel are essential for clinicians to do their jobs. Understanding their needs will require a broadening and deepening of the ways in which organizations listen to their employees. And meeting the needs of personnel will take management skills that combine two attributes that managers may believe conflict with each other—flexibility and reliability.

The Challenge

Data collected from healthcare employees show that burnout has been building as a problem for decades, and the last few years have been crushing—especially for women and minorities. Press Ganey's Employee Engagement Indicator rolls up national data from a wide range of metrics used in surveys of employees in healthcare organizations. In 2021, this indicator declined in every single job category. Overall, the lowest engagement results were seen among clinicians and security workforces, the two frontline groups that were particularly likely to have difficulty decompressing—that is, disconnecting and recharging—after they have gone home.

The data also reflect the positive motivations that remain powerful for most people working in healthcare, and they suggest a viable path forward that should help to build trust. In the analytic model we use at Press Ganey, we think of resilience as a reflection of two different factors we measure separately—activation, a sense of purpose and meaning in their work, and decompression. Despite the stresses of the last few years, and the worsening decompression scores, activation remains largely unchanged and at a high level across every subgroup. (See Table 7.1.)

Table 7.1 Resilience Item Movement (1–5 scale)

Resilience Item	Resilience Theme	2022	2021	Difference
I am able to free my mind from work when I am away from it.	Decompression	3.67	3.74	−0.07
I rarely lose sleep over work issues.	Decompression	3.69	3.76	−0.07
I can enjoy my personal time without focusing on work matters.	Decompression	3.77	3.84	−0.07
I am able to disconnect from work communication during my free time.	Decompression	3.78	3.84	−0.06
My work is meaningful.	Activation	4.47	4.50	−0.03
The work I do makes a real difference.	Activation	4.44	4.42	0.02

(continued)

(continued)

Resilience Item	Resilience Theme	2022	2021	Difference
I see every patient/ client as an individual with specific needs.	Activation	4.56	4.57	−0.01
I care for all patients/ clients equally, even when it is difficult.	Activation	4.57	4.57	0.00

Deeper analyses of those data on about 410,000 employees in 2021 yielded results that were both startling and pleasant (two adjectives that aren't used together very often these days). For different job categories, we identified the most important risk factors indicating a likelihood that an employee would leave. Across the board, these signs related to culture and values. Of course, employees need to be fairly paid and adequately supported, but after these basic needs are met, other factors determine whether they stay or go. (See Table 7.2.)

Table 7.2 Shared Risk Factors Across Roles
(Numbers indicate magnitude of increased risk
multiplication for considering leaving)

Would Stay by Role	Highest Risk Factor (Risk Multiplier)	Second-Highest Risk Factor (Risk Multiplier)	Third-Highest Risk Factor (Risk Multiplier)	Fourth-Highest Risk Factor (Risk Multiplier)	Fifth-Highest Risk Factor (Risk Multiplier)
Nursing (RN)	Organization provides high-quality care (5.4)	Work is meaningful (5.0)	Like the work (5.0)	Job makes good use of skills (4.5)	Business conducted ethically (4.2)

Would Stay by Role	Highest Risk Factor (Risk Multiplier)	Second-Highest Risk Factor (Risk Multiplier)	Third-Highest Risk Factor (Risk Multiplier)	Fourth-Highest Risk Factor (Risk Multiplier)	Fifth-Highest Risk Factor (Risk Multiplier)
Nursing (Other)	The work I do makes a difference (5.9)	Like the work (5.6)	Work is meaningful (5.5)	Organization provides high-quality care (5.4)	See every patient as an individual (4.5)
Clinical Pro	See every patient as an individual (6.9)	Organization provides high-quality care (6.9)	Like the work (6.8)	The work I do makes a difference (5.4)	Job makes good use of skills (5.2)
MD	Job makes good use of skills (5.6)	Organization values diversity (5.5)	Like the work (5.3)	Organization respects caregivers (5.2)	Respect for manager's ability (5.2)
APC	Like the work (8.2)	The work I do makes a difference (8.1)	See every patient as an individual (7.5)	Organization provides high-quality care (6.3)	Business conducted ethically (6.1)
Clerical	See every patient as an individual (7.1)	Like the work (7.0)	Work is meaningful (6.4)	Organization provides high-quality care (6.0)	The work I do makes a difference (5.6)
Licensed Tech	The work I do makes a difference (5.9)	Work is meaningful (5.8)	Like the work (5.6)	Organization provides high-quality care (5.1)	Organization respects caregivers (4.4)

(continued)

(continued)

Would Stay by Role	Highest Risk Factor (Risk Multiplier)	Second-Highest Risk Factor (Risk Multiplier)	Third-Highest Risk Factor (Risk Multiplier)	Fourth-Highest Risk Factor (Risk Multiplier)	Fifth-Highest Risk Factor (Risk Multiplier)
Service	Organization provides high-quality care (5.9)	Like the work (5.5)	The work I do makes a difference (5.5)	Work is meaningful (5.2)	Organization respects caregivers (5.0)
Maintenance	See every patient as an individual (17.1)	Work is meaningful (12.0)	Like the work (8.9)	Organization committed to workplace diversity (8.3)	Organization values diversity (7.9)
Security	See every patient as an individual (6.6)	The work I do makes a difference (6.2)	Organization provides high-quality care (6.1)	Like the work (5.6)	Work is meaningful (5.5)

These findings are not very surprising to managers who rub shoulders with healthcare employees every day and realize that everyone wants to feel good about the work they do, and be proud when they tell neighbors where they work. They also help explain why Press Ganey data consistently show that employee engagement correlates strongly with patient experience, safety, and every other type of performance indicator.

All these data indicate that if leaders can build the type of organization that their employees trust, there is a good chance that positive things will follow. And that process must begin with listening—broadly and deeply.

Listening Broadly to the Workforce

Not many leaders think of themselves as out of touch, but a good number would be nervous about asking their employees for their take. It's clear that the strongest leaders—the ones who generate the most trust—walk the walk. For example, when Covid-19 hit, leaders like Northwell Health's CEO, Michael Dowling, did not retreat to vacation homes; they showed up at every facility and on every shift. And they didn't just walk through the sites where care was being delivered—they stopped, asked what was going wrong and what was going well, and listened. There is no substitute for that kind of visibility when it comes to developing empathy and demonstrating authenticity. But it's not enough.

No matter how wonderful interactions might be during leadership walk rounds, leaders should recognize that they are only interacting with a small percentage of the employees, and the impact of even the most charismatic leader decreases quickly beyond a small circle of impact. The scientific basis for this limitation can be explored by reading about Dunbar's number, which describes the limitations on number of meaningful relationships—the average is about 150—that can be maintained by human beings.[1] As a result, leaders who rely on in-person interactions are at risk of overestimating their grasp of the employee concerns, and they can also have unrealistic notions of how widely their authenticity is appreciated.

Effective senior leaders understand these risks and limitations and know they are amplified through other levels of management. Employees on the front lines should interact with others who reflect the values of the organization and who can listen on behalf of leadership. But beyond creating the equivalent of bucket brigades to carry insights back and forth, organizations need to use new tools to gather feedback from employees. The key words in the preceding sentence are *use* and *new*.

How to Use Tools to Gather Insights

The tools to measure employee engagement yield the best data when they are applied at the right times. They best way to get the most useful data is to:

- **Measure frequently:** A common practice among healthcare organizations in calmer times was to measure employee engagement only once every couple of years. The goal was essentially quality *assurance* rather than quality *improvement.* The purpose was to make sure nothing mortifying was going on, rather than try to improve the current baseline.

    That practice seems to be fading away because recent times have been so unstable that to measure employee engagement only once every two years would be like taking the temperature of a hospitalized patient once a week. Today, the standard practice used by many organizations is to survey the entire workforce at least annually, and use multiple pulse surveys focused on specific issues or directed at specific subsets of the workforce.

- **Measure during crises:** Another misguided practice is delaying surveys until a difficult period is over. The rationale is that the results from challenging times might not be representative of the true perspectives of the workforce. This might have made sense when difficult periods were rare, but today, difficult periods are becoming endemic, like Covid-19 itself. To return to the analogy of vital signs, to delay surveying until a crisis is over is like waiting until a patient has cooled down before taking their temperature. Difficult periods are the moments at which measuring matters most.

- **Share the data:** A major misstep is not sharing employee engagement data after they have been collected. This thinking is not hard to understand, and I can empathize with the leaders who do it. The reasoning is that the data might discourage managers and the rest of the workforce, especially if the problems identified are overwhelming and difficult to respond to.

  The problem is that this misstep undermines trust. Your employees are aware of these problems because they are living with them. They know that a survey was done, and that management thus knows about the problems. When employees take a survey and management does not share the results and act on them, the natural conclusion is that the organization does not really care, or that management lacks the *logic* (using the term from Frances Frei's model of trust) for addressing the problems.

For these reasons, difficult times are the *best* times to measure how things are going for employees, because that is the ideal moment to understand their needs. It is a way of showing that leaders are empathetic and really want to understand the problems. Difficult times are also the best times to demonstrate that leaders are willing to lead the organization, no matter how complex the challenges. Accordingly, the turmoil of the last few years has made it common practice to measure employee sentiments frequently and to share data transparently.

Measuring Employee Engagement with a New Tool

The technology for conducting rapid, pulse surveys has improved tremendously. Managers can write up questions in Microsoft Word and import that file into a tool that converts it into a survey that can be texted or emailed to targeted audiences—all in an hour or less. This functionality is often described as the *self-service* approach to surveying.

Self-service surveys are great, but to get full value from them, organizations will have to determine the right content, create the surveys that they want, send them out, and analyze the data that come back. Another challenge is that benchmark data to put findings in context are unlikely to be available. Thus, in 2021, it would have been impossible to know whether an organization's declines in employee engagement were better, worse, or about the same as those seen in the rest of healthcare. For those reasons, my take is that self-service tools should be seen as complements to, not substitutes for, the use of more traditional engagement surveys that capture data on a wide range of topics and allow more detailed analyses.

Self-service surveying is not the only new tool that organizations can use to build trust in their employees. Technology for conducting online focus groups now employs artificial intelligence (AI) to extract insights from spoken language and even visual cues. Crowd-sourcing applications can be used to engage the people who *really* know the impact of problems (i.e., frontline workers) so their insight can be used to generate and prioritize possible solutions.

In sum, the ability to listen to the workforce more frequently and the tools available to do so are much greater than in the past. Implementing this type of broad listening conveys a message to employees that the organization cares about their problems and intends to address them.

Listening More Deeply

The topics that matter most to employees in healthcare are deeper than salary and the adequacy of staffing support. Press Ganey's analyses over the last few years reveal the importance of more subtle issues, such as understanding whether people feel like they fit in the organization. If they don't feel like they belong, it's hard for them to feel loyal, and they are much more likely to take a job elsewhere.

Groups that are at risk for feeling alienated can be defined by race, ethnicity, gender, and other characteristics. Gathering data by segments is necessary to understand the needs of diverse groups and enable analyses that reveal pain points. For example, Press Ganey data demonstrate that while women physicians spend more time with their patients and more time documenting their work, they are less likely than male physicians to feel they have the time and support they need, and less likely to feel involved in decisions affecting their work. Other data show that the stresses on women physicians at home are greater than those experienced by their male counterparts.

The result is greater burnout among women physicians and a greater risk that they will leave medicine. Treating all physicians the same seems like a reasonable approach, until one realizes that it will cause women physicians to look for the door. The implication is that organizations should be ready to listen deeply to each segment of physicians, and be flexible in coming up with interventions aimed at addressing their unique needs. Those steps will build trust within each segment.

Deeper measuring can uncover deeper psychological concerns that may not be captured by standard survey tools. For example,

Press Ganey's data demonstrate a strong correlation between safety culture and employees' likelihood of staying. But to really grasp what safety means to employees requires understanding the four types of harm described by my colleague Tejal Gandhi:

1. Physical harm

2. Financial harm

3. Emotional and psychological harm

4. Socio-behavioral harm

Patients and employees can encounter all of these, and all four types can occur at any point across the continuum of care. All four can lead to loss of trust by both patients and employees.

The Covid-19 pandemic has demonstrated the importance of this larger concept of safety. Caregivers have felt menaced and even been assaulted by patients and patients' families. They have worried about the availability of PPE, vaccines, tests, and treatments. They have suffered direct and indirect financial blows (e.g., being furloughed or having higher childcare costs). With these issues constantly arising, organizations have to show that they deserve their employees' trust every day—and measuring their employees' current experience in these areas is an essential first step.

To listen deeply to employees, organizations need clarity on what to listen for. Employees have personal issues that shape their trust in their organizations, but they also have issues with the organization. They care about their own welfare, but they also want the organization to make them proud.

That means that it is important to understand employees' fears about issues that might directly affect them, but it is also important to understand their hopes for their organization. How the organization makes employees feel has considerable influence on their desire to stay. A reasonable goal is for organizations to want their employees to feel good when someone asks them, "Where do you work?"

A tool to help move organizations in that direction is appreciative inquiry, an approach that emphasizes the positive rather than the negative. In appreciative inquiry exercises, clinical and nonclinical personnel discuss patient cases in which the care that was delivered made them proud. Then, they try to dissect what characteristics of the case were most important, so they can create a clearer vision of what they would like to make routine. The Cleveland Clinic, for example, has had all employees participate in appreciative inquiry exercises in which managers, health professionals, and support staff mingle at tables of 10.

When healthcare providers' employees perform appreciative inquiry exercises, they *always* highlight care that is well coordinated, compassionate, and timely. The cases reflect on instances in which everyone on the team worked well together to meet the needs of patients, and the patients realized and appreciated it. Because the cases come from the personnel themselves and reflect the care they delivered, the themes that emerge are more compelling than they would be if delivered in a speech by a senior leader or an outside expert.

Responding with Authenticity

Even as leaders/managers generate the basis for empathy by listening to employees, they must demonstrate their authenticity if they are to inspire trust. It is crucial to be authentic, and doing so requires transparency. Leaders and managers must communicate with openness, candor, and repetition. Core values should be stated over and over and over.

Ron Williams, the former CEO of Aetna, observes that leaders must align their actions with their words. "The minute your behavior is different than your words, it's all over," he said. "So you have to make a conscious choice. If you say that you're a values-based organization and you do not start every opportunity to speak to employees, to speak to customers, to speak to clients, to speak to the board, with the values of that organization, then the values are implicitly unimportant."[2]

What values are most important for leaders and managers to make explicit? Just look at the drivers of loyalty by employees in Chapter 4 and earlier in this chapter. Leaders and managers must show that they are truly committed to:

- Zero harm (physical, financial, emotional, and socio-behavioral) for patients *and* for employees

- A culture that treats every patient *and* every employee with respect

- High-quality care and service

- Diversity, equity, and inclusion

Blogs and speeches have their roles, but so do videos and artistic performances. There is a reason to keep in mind the oft-repeated saying: "People will forget what you said and forget what you did, but they will never forget how you made them feel."

The gold standard for expressing the aspirations of a healthcare organization via video is the Cleveland Clinic's "Empathy: The Human Connection to Patient Care." In less than five minutes, with not one spoken word, this video captures the thoughts and emotions of the patients and personnel whose lives intersect in the hallways and rooms of the Cleveland Clinic. The Clinic made this short video on a shoestring budget as a training tool in an effort to remind its personnel of what their patients were enduring. It quickly went viral after it was posted in 2013, and it had more than 6 million views on YouTube as of 2022. Healthcare providers throughout the United States and beyond felt that it captured the reasons they went into the industry.[3]

At the Cleveland Clinic, the video helped create an internal brand embraced by employees. The key leaders in this work included the CEO, Toby Cosgrove, and his close colleague Jim Merlino. Cosgrove also gave out 40,000 lapel buttons that said "Patients First" after he made his first major address to the Cleveland Clinic community. He didn't want there to be any confusion about what value would to guide the organization's choices. And, of course, once leaders make it clear that "Patients First" is the organization's stated value, it becomes next to impossible to make decisions that are in conflict.

Cosgrove decided to use the "Patients First" slogan by shortening what Mayo Clinic calls its primary value, "The needs of the patient come first." That phrase, uttered a century ago by one of the Mayo brothers, is prominent on walls, on stationery letterheads, and on lapel buttons at Mayo. It might look like a marketing slogan to Mayo's first-time visitors, but one cannot help but notice that it comes up constantly in conversation. Mayo employees allude to it as they discuss decisions. They preface their preferences with, "Well, here at Mayo, the needs of that patient come first . . ." as casually as they might say, "Well, here in Rochester, it gets cold in the winter."

There is a subtle but valuable lesson in the impact of the Cleveland Clinic's "Empathy" video and the Mayo Clinic's message that the needs of the patient come first: shared stories and shared values are powerful in building trust and reliability. The fact that the scenes in the Cleveland Clinic video are familiar to everyone who works at that organization, and the fact that the same phrase rolls off tongues in the same cadence at Mayo Clinic demonstrate shared articulations of values that strengthen cultures and build trust among employees. When a Cleveland Clinic employee meets someone who, like them, got choked up at the video's 1:18 mark, when the little girl pets the dog, they are more likely to think, "This person is like me. I can trust them."

To bolster trust and show authenticity, leaders and managers should be transparent about data that reveal challenges, and engage frontline caregivers in finding potential solutions. After all, they are most affected by care-delivery problems and are thus most likely to understand their true impact and suggest logical solutions, but data suggest that their contributions aren't being invited. The survey item "I am involved in decisions that affect my work" elicits higher rates of negative responses from women and minorities, who predominate the ranks of frontline caregivers. This strongly correlates with the likelihood that they are considering leaving the organization.

An example of organizations earning the trust of employees by seeking solutions is the Get Rid of Stupid Stuff (GROSS) program created at Hawaii Pacific Health, described in a *New England Journal of Medicine* article in 2018,[4] and soon replicated at the Cleveland Clinic and other organizations. In starting the GROSS program, leaders at Hawaii Pacific Health acknowledged that there were lots of activities demanded of their employees that added no value to patient care. All these activities, even if they just mean a mouse click or two, take a toll on caregivers.

Hawaii Pacific's leaders won credibility with their employees when they introduced GROSS by acknowledging that many tasks seemed pointless and made staff members wonder, "Why am I doing this?" Even the acronym GROSS, and the implicit message that the last S did not really stand for *stuff*, made employees laugh; it conveyed the message that their leaders had a sense of humor and were actually like them.

Through the GROSS program, employees can use email to identify that certain work is potentially stupid. The tasks are investigated, and many of them turn out to indeed be pointless. One common source of stupid stuff is computerization of a task formerly done on paper. My favorite example was a nomination from an emergency medicine physician about the practice of printing an after-visit summary and then scanning it back into the system after the patient had signed it. It was a procedure left over from the days of paper charts. His email ended with the word *WHY* in capital letters punctuated by a series of exclamation marks. (He was angry.) His query led Hawaii Pacific eliminate this requirement—which delighted that physician and saved time for many other employees.

Responding with Logic

Good intentions are a good start, but they are not enough to build trust among employees during stressful times. Leaders and managers must also have good ideas about how to respond to challenges, and they must be able to communicate their logic to the employees.

The Covid-19 pandemic taught many organizations that the first goal in responding to a crisis is addressing the safety and well-being of the caregiving team. This prioritization may seem in conflict with statements like "Patients First," but the logic is similar to the recommendation given before every commercial air flight—in the case of an emergency in which oxygen masks are deployed, adults traveling with young children should put their masks on before turning to help their children.

In a 2020 *NEJM Catalyst* article, Michael Dowling, the CEO of Northwell, and his colleagues described their Keeping Our Team Members Safe initiative, which prioritized the physical, emotional, financial, and psychosocial safety and well-being of Northwell's employees.[5] In a sense, this initiative had been in development for decades. It originated in response to a fear of terrorist attacks. Northwell, like many other systems, began building a robust emergency preparedness infrastructure. As Dowling put it, "Our basic philosophy was that we must prepare for the unpredictable."

Northwell's emergency operations team includes an incident commander (chief operating officer) and deputy incident commander (chief administrative officer). The team is structured around five categories—operations, clinical operations, finance and administration, logistics, and planning, which included a special subgroup focused on the well-being of employees.

Northwell made the decision to survey its employees repeatedly throughout the Covid-19 pandemic. For example, they surveyed about 70,000 employees from May 4 to May 11, 2020, which was an early, difficult time in the Covid-19 pandemic in New York, where Northwell is located. Within one week, 24,708 employees responded. Of the respondents, 35 percent requested resources for managing stress or psychological well-being—the single greatest need across all job categories. Employees also requested resources for caring for their overall well-being (31 percent), physical well-being (29 percent), and caretaking responsibilities (23 percent). Physicians requested support in navigating Northwell processes.

In response, Northwell's leaders gathered data during some of the darkest hours and were transparent in publishing it inside and outside the organization. And they did not search for a magic bullet to address the well-being of their workforce. Instead, they developed a multidimensional initiative in response to the data.

In his article describing the initiative, Dowling acknowledged "we faced four major hurdles: cost, time, political will, and evaluation." Estimating costs was next-to-impossible; every week represented uncharted territory. Developing, communicating, and implementing the programs consumed huge amounts of management time.

One of the many metrics Northwell tracked was workforce retention rates—which actually improved 18 percent between March and July 2020. Leadership sensed that they were on the right track. They expanded their measurement program from surveying all employees and physicians once a year, to conducting an additional pulse survey of 30 percent of employees and targeted micro-pulse surveys, each with a focus on one key area.

One of those targeted surveys—of personnel working remotely in July 2020—found that 87 percent thought that Northwell cared about their well-being during the pandemic, and 95 percent believed that Northwell transparently communicated information regarding Covid-19. The basic principles of measuring, responding, and being transparent are now integrated into Northwell's long-term approach to building trust among its employees.

Diversity and Trust

Diversity, equity, and inclusion (DEI) will be addressed at greater length in Chapter 9, but its importance for building trust among employees must be noted here. A basic building block of a trusting culture is confidence among all employees that they will be treated with respect. In the pursuit of that social norm, excellence requires the same high-reliability frame of mind for interactions with colleagues. In that frame of mind, people know they are starting from scratch every day; excellence means being at one's best with the next patient one sees or the next colleague with whom one interacts.

But inspiring trust requires more than making respect a social norm. It also requires demographic diversity at every level, including senior management. The painful reality is that senior management in most healthcare organizations looks demographically like C-suites in other business sectors—predominantly white and male.

These senior managers may be unbiased and inclusive as individuals, but the reality is that people in minority groups are constantly wondering, "Is there anyone here who looks like me?" That question does not occur to people who are part of the majority subset, and occurs only intermittently to those who come from privileged socioeconomic backgrounds. But it occurs all the time to everyone else. And it is harder for someone to trust an organization where they aren't sure that anyone grasps what their life is like.

Another important step in building trust is anticipation of those rare but horrible moments in which patients or their visitors make offensive comments to staff. For example, occasionally patients have demanded a different caregiver because of racial or ethnic prejudice, or have made derogatory comments about a caregiver's religion. When these episodes occur, the tendency of other caregivers is to freeze in disbelief, unsure of what to do or say. The person who is the target of the offensive comment tends to leave the room, feeling like the organization does not have their back.

Some organizations have developed protocols and scripts (sometimes printed on laminated cards) for handling these situations.[6] The scripts usually convey the message to the patient or visitor that their message is unacceptable at the institution, and arrangements will be made to transfer their care elsewhere as soon as it is medically safe.

The following is distributed to all patients seeking care at Well-Span Health, the integrated delivery system in central Pennsylvania and northern Maryland:

Respect and Consideration

We trust that our patients, their families and visitors, share our commitment to treating all physicians, advanced practice providers, staff, and other persons in this care location with the dignity and respect that they deserve.

As a patient, family member or guardian, we expect that you:

- Recognize and respect the rights of other patients, families and staff. Any threatening, violent or harassing behavior exhibited toward other patients, visitors and/ or care location staff for any reason, including based on age, sex, race, color, religion, sexual orientation, gender identification, national origin, ancestry, culture, language, veteran status, disability or other aspects of difference will be considered discriminatory and will not be tolerated.

- Understand that the care location will attempt to accommodate a patient's choice of care giver whenever possible, however, we cannot accommodate a patient's choice of care giver, or refusal of treatment, based upon the care giver's ethic background, religion, national origin, or other discriminating factors. The patient's refusal to be treated, under these circumstances, may result in transfer of the patient's care to another facility. Also, in the event of an emergency, patients may receive treatment by any qualified physician or healthcare professional, regardless of patient preference.[7]

WellSpan also developed standard workflows and recommended language for situations in which patients ask for caregivers of a different race. I have not seen any data on how often these scripts have been used and what effect they have had on interactions, but it seems clear that the development of these scripts helps build the sense among caregivers that they can trust their organization and colleagues.

In sum, improving DEI is the right thing to do. It is also an operational imperative, given the increased risk that employees who rate the organization low on inclusiveness will leave. To build real trust, organizations should convey the message, "We not only respect you here, we value you and we will support you in the face of injustice."

Incentives

Money is not the most important thing to people working in healthcare, but it still matters, and acting as if it is not important at all erodes trust. Even though data indicate that employees' sense that their compensation is fair is only weakly correlated with their likelihood of leaving the organization, the fact is that there is a correlation. And the percentage of employees who are concerned about the fairness of their compensation is considerably higher than the percentage who have considerations that are associated with a greater risk of leaving, such as the organization's commitment to quality. Compensation is thus an important risk factor for losing employees, even if it is not a powerful risk factor.

Incentive programs are of intense interest to employees, even when the actual financial stakes are small compared to their base salaries. This means that incentive programs can be harmful to employees' trust if they are not carefully designed. This dynamic is consistent with prospect theory (also known as loss-aversion theory), the behavioral economics work that won Daniel Kahneman the Nobel Prize in Economics in 2002.

This theory, developed with the late Amos Tversky, describes how people fear losses more than they value gains. For example, their studies showed that the pain of losing $100 is roughly comparable to the positive effects of gaining $200. They also showed that people value small losses or gains out of proportion with their actual amount. If you give someone $200, they are happier than if you gave them $100, but not twice as happy.[8]

The takeaway message for the design of incentive programs is that small incentive packages framed as potential losses yield the

greatest impact for the incentive dollar. For example, telling someone that their salary will be $60,000, but they will lose $200 for
each of five performance targets that they fail to reach is a more
powerful motivation than telling them their salary will be $59,000,
but they can earn an additional $200 for hitting each of five targets.
The offer is the same, but the second is more appealing because
people hate to lose what they consider to be theirs.

While potential losses are highly motivating, incentive programs can erode trust for the very reason that they work—people
hate to lose money. If the incentives are intended to promote
behaviors that employees believe are the right things to do (e.g.,
improve quality), it usually takes very little money to have an
impact. But when employees compare incentives, they are likely to
doubt the fairness of measuring and allocating them, to the detri-
ment of trust. The damage is even greater when the incentives are
designed to promote behaviors that are not related to the quality
of care.

For this reason, nonfinancial incentives are often better options
for promoting quality of care. Many leading organizations like
Mayo Clinic, the Cleveland Clinic, and Kaiser Permanente put
employees on straight salary, and do not include direct financial
incentives for any type of performance. Others have a strong productivity incentive for physicians but nonfinancial incentives (peer
pressure) for quality and other nonfinancial issues. Still others use
financial incentives for both productivity and quality.

There is no perfect incentive system for all organizations. On
the one hand, organizations that don't use financial incentives usually have very strong organizational cultures, so peer pressure is
effective for achieving almost any performance goal. On the other
hand, in most organizations, financial incentives for performance
goals are useful and often necessary to draw attention to work of
strategic importance.

My colleagues at Press Ganey and I hear about missteps in incentive programs with some regularity, in part because angry employees (especially physicians) often begin by blaming the data rather than the incentive system. These experiences have allowed us to develop expertise in mistakes to be avoided.

In general, for physician performance, we recommend that financial incentives be team-based, such as for a group of clinic staff with the same subspecialty or a team of hospitalists. We recommend rewarding improvement and thus fostering a growth mindset rather than reaching some arbitrary goal. And we recommend that the external context be considered. For example, Covid-19 created a negative trajectory in patient experience throughout the country, and incentives based upon improvement were likely to be lost, leading to disappointment.

We get so many questions about incentives that my colleague Deirdre Mylod led the development of responses to the following frequently asked questions related to physician incentive programs. Adhering to these recommendations and adapting them for non-physicians will, we think, enhance organizations' likelihood of accelerating improvement without compromising their employees' trust.

Choosing Measures

To choose the most effective incentive measures, consider the following:

Are Other Incentives Already in Place for This Outcome?

Many health plans have incentives created for physicians based upon patient experience measures. When provider organizations establish goals and incentives, they should be aware of the broader landscape impacting clinicians. Ideally, a single source of truth should be established so that clinicians have clear insight into how their performance is being measured and so they are not expected to manage multiple sets of outcomes. If the same data cannot be used in all cases, programs should be aligned to the greatest extent possible in terms of their measures and incentives. Clinicians should be provided with clear information regarding the source of the metrics, how goals are established, and what expectations have been set across the programs that impact their work.

Recommendation: Align or harmonize measures across incentive programs as much as possible. If different measures are used, or different goals are set, provide clarity about those definitions and how they relate to each other.

Are Incentives for Other Domains of Quality Outcomes Already in Place for These Individuals?

What other domains of quality (e.g., safety, quality, productivity, etc.) have incentives in place that impact these same individuals? How are goals and performance thresholds determined for these other areas? When considering incentives for patient-experience metrics, are you using a similar framework for decision-making and recommendations? If different approaches are used, can the rationale and benefit of doing so be clearly articulated?

Recommendation: Align or harmonize your methods of creating incentive programs as much as possible across various domains of quality and performance. If different approaches or strategies are used, provide explanations regarding the need for or benefits of the disparate approaches.

Are the Measures You Are Using Asking About Interactions with the Doctor or Clinician?

Some questions on CAHPS or Press Ganey surveys ask about patient attitudes related to the overall brand (e.g., likelihood to recommend the hospital or clinic), general interactions with staff (e.g., staff worked together to care for you), or process-related issues (e.g., ease of scheduling, wait times). Other measures ask patients to evaluate the interaction they had with specific groups of personnel, such as nurses or physicians.

Recommendation: When working on physician or clinician performance, use measures that ask specifically about interactions with the doctor or clinician caring for the patient.

Are the Measures You Are Using Specific to an Individual?

In the medical practice setting, the care provider questions specifically refer to the one person the patient saw during their visit. But on the inpatient survey (e.g., HCAHPS or Press Ganey Inpatient), the questions refer broadly to interactions with doctors (plural) rather than interactions with a specific doctor, and they ask for a summary of the experience across all interactions with all doctors.

Note that the Centers for Medicare & Medicaid Services (CMS) specifically cautions against using HCAHPS measures to compare or assess individual staff members:

> HCAHPS scores are designed and intended for use at the hospital level for the comparison of hospitals. CMS does not review or endorse the use of HCAHPS scores for comparisons within hospitals, such as comparison of HCAHPS scores associated with a particular ward, floor, individual staff member, etc. to others. Such comparisons are unreliable unless large sample sizes are collected at the ward, floor, or individual staff member level. In addition, since HCAHPS questions inquire about broad categories of hospital staff (such as doctors in general and nurses in general, rather than specific individuals), HCAHPS is not appropriate for comparing or assessing individual staff members. Using

HCAHPS scores to compare or assess individual staff members is inappropriate and strongly discouraged by CMS.[9]

Recommendation: When choosing measures, ensure they relate to interactions with the intended individual rather than a team or group of staff.

Accurate Attribution

To ensure the at the data can be accurately attributed, consider the following:

Can You Accurately Attribute Survey Data to an Individual?

Most organizations will fill in a value for a code relating to the attending physician or for the physician seen in a clinic. But sometimes those attributions do not completely reflect who cared for the patient.

Recommendation: Ensure that when you assign a patient to a clinician, you confirm that the assignment is accurate.

Can the Patient Identify the Single Person Who Is Being Evaluated?

In the medical practice setting, the patient has an appointment with a particular person and can reasonably be expected to be specific when asked to evaluate that particular person. In the inpatient setting, patients are cared for by many physicians, hospitalists, specialists, and so on. Inpatient surveys typically are not designed to ask patients about one particular person (e.g., one out of several hospitalists), and patients may have a difficult time recalling each individual clinician by name.

Recommendation: Ensure the patient will unambiguously know who you are asking them to evaluate.

Is It Advisable to Attribute Performance to a Team Rather Than an Individual?

Though many organizations create incentive programs that are specific to individuals, team-based goals can be even more powerful. Aggregating results to a team (e.g., clinicians with the same subspecialty or clinicians within the same clinic) can mitigate other methodological concerns such as attribution and n-size issues, and can also appeal to the sense of teamwork that is critical for patient's experience and staff's well-being.

Recommendation: Consider team-based incentives in lieu of clinician-specific goals.

Accuracy of Results

To maximize the accuracy of your data, consider the following:

Is Your n-Size Large Enough?

In the early days of surveying, when questionnaires were delivered only by mail or over the phone, it could be difficult to achieve a robust sample size for each clinician. With the advent of digital surveys and email or text methodologies, organizations have cost-effective means of achieving a high number of responses for each individual. Statistical guides suggest 30 responses as the bare minimum to provide meaningful data, however such a sample size still has considerable error. Establishing a minimum of 50 or higher will reduce error and create more precision in measurement.

Recommendation: Organizations should be very clear about the minimum number of surveys needed to evaluate a clinician, and they should discuss that target number with clinician leaders as part of designing a measurement program.

Are You Leveraging Specialty-Specific Benchmarking to Understand the Context of Performance Goals?

There are normative differences in scores based on the specialty of the physician. Different types of patients have different needs, their cases have different levels of complexity, and they face vastly different concerns. The same score could rank in the upper quartile for one specialty, but fall below the median for another.

Recommendation: Specialty-specific benchmarking should be used to identify what *high performance* means within each clinical cohort.

Goal Setting

To set goals that not only provide benchmarks for success but also help set priorities, increase motivation, and foster teamwork, consider the following:

Were Physician Leaders Involved in the Process of Goal Setting?

Most organizations document the definitional elements of their physician incentive programs so that they can be transparent about the goals they have established. It's also critical to be transparent about the process of establishing those goals. Physician leaders should be at the table from the beginning so that they are included in decision-making that impacts incentive programs.

Recommendation: Involve physician leaders in the process of designing incentive programs.

Are Goals and Incentives Established Based on Individual Improvement over Baseline Rather Than a Threshold Level of Performance That Everyone Must Achieve?

Often, goals require all individuals to achieve the same outcome (e.g., a score of 80 percent Top Box or the 75th percentile within their own specialty). Setting goals in this way assumes that everyone has the same likelihood of achieving it by optimizing interactions with patients.

We know that some types of patients (e.g., younger patients, female patients) are less likely to report optimal care experiences. We are also beginning to see that, due to their background or identity, some clinicians may experience bias from patients.

Improvement-based goals, rather than threshold-based goals, can mitigate the impact of bias and variation in panels. Improvement-based goals can be operationalized by establishing that everyone in this specialty who is currently at this level of performance will be asked to improve by X amount (either a score improvement or a rank improvement).

Recommendation: Use improvement-based goals to support a growth mindset and prevent bias from adversely impacting clinicians.

Was the Goal for Improvement Set Based on Reasonable and Attainable Estimates of Improvement?

Organizations often confuse aspirations with annual goal setting. Aspirational performance levels can be incorporated into a vision statement for what the future might look like, but annual goals should be set based on improvement that is reasonable and achievable.

Each year, Press Ganey assesses the actual pace of improvement across our databases to determine the probability of an organization achieving various levels of improvement. Importantly, these projections of improvement take into account the starting level of performance. Organizations that are already in the top decile (above the 90th percentile) are less likely to see further increases in performance, while those starting at the 20th percentile typically see larger gains year over year.

Recommendation: Use national data to understand reasonable rates of annual improvement given where your organization is today.

Are Incentives Scaled So Continuous Improvement Is Encouraged?

Using a single target to determine goal attainment may disincentivize the larger objective of continuous improvement. If an individual does not feel close enough to reaching the target, they may give up or withdraw effort. Those who know they have already hit their number may feel they have achieved what is necessary and do not need to press forward. Scaling incentives by establishing tiers of goals associated with different levels of reinforcement can mitigate this concern and promote engagement and efforts to improve.

Recommendation: Create incentives that encourage continuous effort and reward performance that approaches or exceeds the goal—not just performance that attains the goal.

Clinician Wellness

To balance clinician well-being with efforts to improve the patient experience, consider the following strategies.

When Improvements in Patient Experience Were Requested of Physicians, Were There Concurrent Efforts to Improve Their Working Conditions and Processes?

Asking physicians to improve their performance without offering support can have a negative effect on their well-being and morale.

This is particularly true if physicians have requested changes to processes or working conditions. For example, streamlining the electronic health record (EHR) and reducing friction points in processes can help physicians reach their goals, and these efforts also support strategic organizational goals. Consider the feedback physicians have given on surveys or via other means of communication and be responsive to their concerns. When physicians have a role in improvement efforts, they are more likely to succeed.

Recommendation: Ensure physician engagement is foundational to any improvement efforts.

Have You Considered the Needs of Physician Wellness in Light of the Need to Improve Patient Experience?

It is important to consider how the needs of patients, physicians, and the organization will be balanced, and how to ensure that patient experience data are not used punitively. Then, clarify what will be done to support their wellness. For example, consider systematically providing physicians with positive comments from patients, or de-emphasizing patient experience goals when setting crisis care standards.

Recommendation: Ensure patient experience data are not used as punishment and are leveraged for positives as well as negatives.

Organizing to Build Employee Trust

The importance of retaining employees and addressing the threats to their trust are so great that organizations have put these issues at the top of their priority list during the Covid-19 pandemic, and current human resources data suggest that they will remain a top priority for the foreseeable future. These dynamics have increased the importance of the chief human resources officer (HRO) in most healthcare organizations, and other members of the senior management team have become immersed in these issues, too.

Some organizations are appointing chief wellness officers (CWOs) and incorporating them in their emergency command structures.[10] Key CWO contributions include identifying evolving sources of worker anxiety, deploying support resources, and participating in operational decision-making. I don't see those contributions diminishing in importance any time soon, so don't expect these roles to go away.

Still, as is true of critical characteristics such as the safety of care, every leader and manager must feel that building trust among employees is a critical part of their job. Ownership must begin with the CEO but be transmitted down to every frontline manager. And every employee should want their colleagues to trust them, and to trust their colleagues in return. Adhering to the principles of being an HRO, every employee should apply these standards to all their interactions with colleagues.

That sounds aspirational, rhetorical, and perhaps overly idealistic. But it should be the clear goal, just like zero harm is the goal for safety. Trust has always been a goal in healthcare, but the last few years have broadened and deepened our understanding of what that means.

CHAPTER 8

Broader and Deeper Safety

THE MEANING OF excellence in safety evolved rapidly during the Covid-19 pandemic. First, hardly anyone takes safety for granted anymore. It has been a period in which patients and caregivers have felt vulnerable, and safety has become a much more important driver of trust in healthcare organizations. Second, concerns about vulnerability extended beyond physical harm to include financial, emotional, and socio-behavioral harm. Third, there has been a deepening of our insights about what makes people feel safe or unsafe.

The surge in the sense of vulnerability was justified, and it was accompanied by an actual increase in safety events. This combination of heightened concern and actual decline in safety was different from the deterioration of financial performance at most healthcare organizations. The financial deficits were painful but they were also situational, and government aid mitigated financial losses due to elective-surgery shutdowns and decreases in office visits. But government assistance cannot regain lost trust among patients and employees.

For safety, the pandemic was like an unsettling audit; it unmasked weaknesses with long-term implications. The increases in safety events came after two decades of improvement for about half of the events tracked in the National Healthcare Quality and Disparities Report from 2000 to 2018.[1] The general sense had been that we had a long way to go in patient safety, but we were making progress. The pandemic has jolted organizations out of any sense of complacency that may have been settling in.

For each type of safety event that increased in frequency, there was a logical explanation. For example, falls occurred because family members weren't there to help unsteady patients make their way to the restroom. Patients who were being proned could not have their lines changed, increasing their risk of infection. A case could be made that, as with financial performance, safety would revert to normal after the pandemic was over, and improvement would resume. But for organizations with a commitment to the goal of zero harm, the honest assessment is that the pandemic revealed weaknesses that might be exposed whenever disruptions occur. We can use the lessons learned during the pandemic to build a more resilient healthcare system that can protect patients and employees from harm, no matter what turmoil arises.[2]

This chapter will discuss three major types of change that are critical to future excellence and trust:

1. How thinking about safety has changed

2. How the work of improving safety has broadened in scope to include the full continuum of care

3. How that work has also deepened to include the prevention of fear

It will conclude with the implications for the work of leaders and managers.

Thinking Differently About Safety

This isn't the first time that thinking about safety has changed in the memories of experienced healthcare leaders. A few decades ago, medical errors that caused harm were assumed to be rare, and the medical malpractice system was considered adequate to address the consequences. Safety was taken for granted, and most healthcare leaders didn't think much about safety at all.

But that changed around the turn of the century, when the Institute of Medicine (IOM) reports disseminated research showing that potentially preventable adverse events (PPAEs) were startlingly common. It took several years for healthcare leaders to fully absorb the implications of the IOM reports and their own safety data, but eventually many organizations committed to the goal of zero harm and started their journeys to becoming high-reliability organizations (HROs).

In the early years of this century, the focus of safety improvement work was preventing physical harm to hospitalized patients. In the last several years, however, thinking about safety has changed in two important ways. The first is an increase in complexity of the definition of harm. The second is understanding of how safety is intertwined with other dimensions of performance (e.g., patient experience and equity). Both types of changes have accelerated in the last few years.

The increase in complexity of the definition of harm is well summarized in a landmark article by my colleague Tejal Gandhi and her coauthors from the Institute for Healthcare Improvement, published in February 2020 just as the Covid-19 pandemic was gaining momentum.[3] They noted that, in addition to *physical* harm, people were vulnerable to *financial* harm, *emotional and psychological* harm, and *socio-behavioral* harm. Financial harm comes from the loss of income or an increase in expenses. Emotional and psychological harm includes loss of dignity and respect, as well as the guilt, shame, and depression suffered by caregivers when involved in harming a patient. Socio-behavioral harms lead to distrust, poor evaluations of care, and unwillingness to return to the healthcare facility (e.g., patients' perception that their pain is not taken seriously by caregivers because of their race or ethnicity).

The sweeping nature of these four types of harm explains why safety can no longer be seen as an isolated silo in healthcare performance. Harm occurs across the continuum of care and can only be addressed by a total systems approach. Gandhi and her coauthors described the need for four interrelated elements: (1) change management (especially attending to the psychology of change), (2) a culture of safety, (3) a learning system, and (4) patient engagement and codesign of care.

The huge investment of leadership energy in this work is justified because data demonstrate what common sense would suggest—that all four types of safety are intertwined with each other and other types of performance. Organizations with stronger safety cultures usually have superior patient experience, higher levels of workforce retention, and better performance in every way.

The result is that thinking about safety has evolved from preventing physical harm to developing a culture obsessed with high reliability on multiple forms of excellence. It should be considered a safety event anytime care deviates from the way it ought to be. Organizations should acknowledge this and study how to prevent such events from recurring. The experience of the last few years should bolster their confidence that their cultures can move in this direction quickly when the need is clear.

Broader Safety

Hospitalized patients are especially vulnerable to physical harm because they are often frail and experience many procedures and treatments. However, the fact is that all four types of harm occur not only in hospitals but across the continuum of care, and the work to improve safety should have that same reach. Fortunately, integrated delivery systems that take clinical and financial responsibility for patients over time (as opposed to just during visits or hospitalizations) are increasingly prominent in US healthcare, yet they all have a lot of work to do to address safety across the continuum.

The most immediate issue is extending the same pursuit of zero harm that many institutions apply within hospitals to ambulatory care and virtual interactions. Doing so requires creating the infrastructure to detect and analyze safety events that occur in these settings and performing root-cause analyses that extend beyond the boundaries of the organization. Safety teams in many hospitals limit the application of root-cause analysis to events that are "under their control," which can exclude problems that occur before or after discharge from the hospital. That perspective clearly is out of date, but relatively few organizations have robust systems for capturing and analyzing safety events experienced by outpatients and after virtual visits. The payoff for investing in such systems is considerable, though. For example, readmission reduction programs include interventions on the social environment of patients after they go home. These have a much greater impact than interventions that focus only on the care delivered by clinicians in the hospital.

Once they've taken responsibility for safety across the continuum of care, healthcare delivery systems should acknowledge that patients can be harmed during the diagnostic process. The care processes during that period are highly variable, and risks include inaccurate diagnoses, confusion, or delays that lead to emotional distress or disease progression.

In the past, most organizations have not focused on improving diagnostic processes, but this period truly matters to patients, and is a way for organizations to differentiate themselves from their competition. For example, Mayo Clinic has long been known for its ability to assemble a team of clinicians around a patient with an uncertain diagnosis and arrive at a treatment plan within a few days. In less organized systems, that same patient might have bounced around without getting any diagnosis or treatment plan. The difference is that Mayo Clinic recognizes that rapid and effective diagnosis is an important safety goal.

Deeper Safety

Deeper safety means working to understand and prevent patient suffering that occurs on a more subtle level than physical pain. Fear is a form of suffering, and experiencing preventable fear should be considered a safety event. We now have a tool to recognize when a patient is becoming fearful. Artificial intelligence and natural language processing (AI/NLP) can be used to analyze patients' comments and identify the causes of fear that are most common or powerful. Thus, failing to ameliorate preventable fear constitutes an error.

Senem Guney and coauthors analyzed 34,552 patient comments obtained during the early days of the Covid-19 pandemic to gain insight into what causes and relieves patient suffering.[4] The patients offered expressions of awareness and gratitude for caregiver professionalism under challenging circumstances. For example, they took note of physicians' explanations for why they could not shake hands with them—and expressed appreciation. But patients also expressed concerns about the cleanliness of the care setting and the hygiene practices of care providers. When patients talk about cleanliness, they describe the staff's handwashing; the availability of masks, hand sanitizers, and wipes; and how objects in the care setting posed threats to hygiene (e.g., "nasty germ-covered iPads defeat[ing] the purpose of trying to be hygienic in the first place"). One insight that emerged during the Covid-19 pandemic was seeing splatters of body fluids on the scrubs and white coats of clinicians is unnerving to patients. The same is true when patients' own gowns or linens are splattered and not quickly replaced.

AI/NLP can be applied to narrower issues and smaller populations to get insight into what raises safety concerns for them. For example, such data can show that patients may be unnerved by confusion and changes of plans right before surgery, concerned that the clinicians performing their procedures are inexperienced trainees, or troubled that the information they received as part of the discharge process was inadequate.

These different types of fears are like near-miss safety events; they may not have caused physical harm, but they warrant identification, reporting, analysis, and prevention. They are different from near-misses, however, in that they do cause harm (i.e., fear). For this reason, AI/NLP analyses conducted at a patient unit level to detect opportunities to improve safety by reducing fear are likely to be part of excellence in the future.

Implications

The changes described above have major implications for leaders and managers in healthcare. The first is that the goal of zero harm must be more than an aspiration for hospitals. It applies to the entire healthcare continuum, and extending it to ambulatory care and telemedicine is a critical medium-term goal.

Asserting new goals at a time when most people in healthcare feel overwhelmed and burned out is not something to be done lightly, but there are business as well as clinical imperatives that make zero harm a priority. Safety events in any setting are dispiriting for caregivers and hasten departures from the workforce.

Moreover, Press Ganey data demonstrate that patient perceptions of safety have become make-or-break drivers of their loyalty.

Press Ganey offers a custom item that can be added to ambulatory patient-experience surveys asking patients about how safe they felt during their care: "How well the staff protected your safety (by washing hands, wearing ID, etc.)." Analyses of over 12 million responses from a national sample of medical practices during 2021 found that 83 percent of patients had no safety concerns (i.e., gave a *top-box* rating). The score for "likelihood to recommend the practice" for this group of patients would rank in the 99th percentile. But 17 percent of patients did not give a top-box rating for their perception of safety, and, among those patients, the score for "likelihood to recommend the practice" was in the 1st percentile. Only 32 percent of patients experiencing suboptimal safety gave a top-box rating to "likelihood to recommend."

When my analyst colleagues focused on the subset of patients who gave their care providers (usually a physician, sometimes a nurse practitioner) top ratings for caring behaviors, safety perception had a similarly dramatic impact. If there were no safety concerns, likelihood to recommend was in the 99th percentile. But if there *were* safety concerns, their "likely to recommend" scores were in the 2nd percentile. In short, patient reservations about the safety of their care can wash away the positive impact of wonderful interactions with their clinicians.

The takeaway is that practices should be measuring patient perceptions of safety in all settings, analyzing comments to understand the root causes of patients' reservations, and applying high-reliability principles and processes to ensure that learning and improvement are happening.

A second implication of the changes described in this chapter is that safety must be more than an array of programs to prevent physical harm; it must be something systemic and cultural.

This implication is particularly concerning given recent trends in safety culture data gleaned from Press Ganey surveys of employees of healthcare organizations. After modest but steady improvement from 2017 to 2019, scores for most safety culture themes declined in 2020, with the most marked drop occurring in the categories of "Prevention & Reporting" and "Resources & Teamwork."

Even before the pandemic, Tejal Gandhi and other safety experts were voicing concerns that improvements in safety culture weren't happening fast enough. And then, when Covid-19 hit, some organizations and some patient-care teams buckled under the strain.

Here's an example from a well-regarded hospital that I won't identify: An elderly woman who had a prolonged hospitalization became malnourished and developed large decubitus ulcers. When this adverse event was identified and root-cause analysis was performed, she was found to have lost 25 pounds during her hospitalization, but the weight loss had gone undetected even though the patient had been ordered to have daily weigh-ins upon admission. The explanation: the nurses on that floor had been stretched so thin that they made informal decisions about which orders to follow and which to ignore. Daily weigh-ins fell into the latter category, day after day after day.

The conclusion drawn at this hospital and many others is that the recent decline in safety culture needs urgent attention. Events like this one reveal more than a problem with weighing patients daily; they reveal a weakly embedded safety culture. And the impact of such events goes beyond the physical harm to patients to the psychological damage to caregivers who cannot do all they know they ought to.

A third major implication is that the phrase "safety is a systems issue" must move from rhetoric to reality. Healthcare delivery systems that include hospitals, outpatient care, and other care-delivery components aggregate financial performance, develop strategies for improvement, and mitigate business risk. They must also approach safety in the same methodical way if they are to build trust among patients and their employees.

This means that the organizations must demonstrate that they are worthy of trust, which requires more than good intentions. It requires real steps (again, *logic* in the Frances Frei framework) to hardwire resilience into the organization. And attaining resilience is impossible without creating an organizational culture of learning. The last chapter of this book will go deeper into resilience thinking and learning cultures.

A fourth and final implication of recent changes is that the era of paternalism in patient safety should be officially declared over. In the past, healthcare leaders tended to be very cautious about what they revealed to the public and to their employees about safety problems. This attitude was justified by concerns that isolated events would be blown out of proportion or misunderstood.

But today, patients and employees have a heightened concern about their exposure to of all four types of harm described by Tejal Gandhi and her coauthors. To gain their trust, healthcare organizations must show their authenticity and the logic of their plans. And that requires transparency of the data, and engaging patients and employees in developing responses.

CHAPTER 9

Diversity, Equity, and Inclusion as Social Capital

THE MURDER OF George Floyd in May 2020 prompted an examination of the nature and impact of inequity throughout society. That process is still underway in healthcare, but this much is clear—equity is an essential part of excellence. It is not a nice-to-have; it is a must-have.

Care cannot be considered excellent if there are technical mishaps or if patients don't have the peace of mind that comes from believing that their outcomes are as good as possible given the cards that they have been dealt. And that means care cannot be considered excellent unless every patient feels that they are respected, that they are believed, that their needs are understood, and that everyone is working together to meet those needs. Achieving that ambitious goal is not possible unless employees in the healthcare workforce feel the same way.

The aspiration of making every patient and every employee feel respected, credible, and valued has been a fuzzy ideal in the past, but now advancing toward that goal has become an operational imperative. Equity is a core value analogous to safety. Zero harm is widely recognized as the right goal for safety; similarly, zero inequity is the right goal for relationships with patients and employees.

Not everyone is comfortable with goals like zero harm or zero inequity. The argument is that goals that seem impossible, such as perfection, are too easy to ignore. However, consider the argument articulated by Vince Lombardi, the legendary Green Bay Packers football coach: "Perfection is not attainable, but if we chase perfection we can catch excellence."

Healthcare organizations have a powerful business incentive to chase perfection in diversity, equity, and inclusion (DEI). As described earlier in this book, there is a strong and consistent correlation between the perceptions clinicians and other healthcare employees have of their organization's DEI, and their overall engagement and likelihood of leaving for another job. Employee engagement is also strongly correlated with how the organization's patients view the quality of their care. In short, data overwhelmingly support improving DEI as a core activity for building trust among patients and employees.

The message that emerges from analyses of data from patients, employees, safety reporting, and business metrics is that healthcare organizations should think of DEI as a form of social capital. Social capital is akin to financial capital—the monetary resources that enable organizations to do things they otherwise could not do. Similarly, improving DEI enables organizations to do things they could not otherwise do. Poor DEI likely dooms organizations to poor performance.

Improving DEI doesn't require enormous investments of financial capital, but it does require leadership, commitment, discipline, and the management infrastructure to monitor and drive progress. It requires thinking clearly about DEI. It also requires thinking differently about it than in the past. To improve DEI, organizations must consider it more broadly and more deeply, and adopt measurement strategies that support this level of thinking.

Thinking Clearly About DEI

The phrase "diversity, equity, and inclusion" has rolled quickly off many tongues in healthcare for years, including my own. These words are not synonyms for one another—and understanding the differences is critical for the work of improving them. They overlap, but progress on one does not mean progress on all three. Understanding how they build upon each other is important for improving them all.

Diversity is about the *who* in the organization. It can be defined as the myriad ways in which people differ in characteristics and experiences at the individual, organizational, institutional, or societal level. Measuring diversity focuses on characteristics such as race, ethnicity, gender, religion, socioeconomic status, age, physical or mental abilities, and nationality or national origin.

Diversity started to become a focus for improvement in many organizations in the 1990s, in part because it was considered a marker of fairness and evidence of equal opportunity. But now diversity is understood to be a powerful influence on the culture and the perspectives of any group. No matter what good intentions people hold, they all have blind spots. Diversity reduces the risk of collective blind spots—assuming, that is, that everyone has a voice and feels free to speak out. Thus, diversity is something that can be measured quantitatively, but its potential to improve organizations is not guaranteed by any specific demographic distribution.

Inclusion is about *what* people experience. Do they feel welcome? Do they feel valued? Do they feel that their talents are recognized and used? Measuring inclusion focuses on whether respondents feel a sense of belonging, believe that the organization has a culture in which differences are accepted, and report that power dynamics do not determine the course of discussions and other interactions.

Inclusion became an increasingly important focus within many organizations in the early years of this century, in part due to recognition that modest improvements in quantifiable diversity were not enough to change organizational cultures. In healthcare, for example, women now comprise the majority in many types of jobs, but data nevertheless demonstrate that they rate the inclusion of their organizations lower than their male counterparts. Improving inclusion requires allowing individuals to fully participate in decision-making in a way that they share power.

Equity is about *how* people are valued. A working definition is "providing access and resources to individuals or groups in a way that accommodates their differences." Think of equity as the workforce equivalent of patient-centered care.

A critical distinction that people understand much better today than before 2020 is the difference between *equality* and *equity*. Equality is treating everyone the same. Equity requires more than that; it requires understanding the root causes of outcome differences, and then being willing and effective in taking them on. It can only be measured by asking individuals about how they perceive the fairness with which they are treated. Are they given opportunities that compensate for prior injustice? And, ultimately, are they treated with respect?

Thinking Differently About DEI

In the summer of 2020, my colleague Tejal Gandhi said to me three or four times, "Equity is like safety." I will admit that I did not immediately get it. I nodded politely and thought to myself that this well-known expert on safety probably thought *everything* was like safety.

Subsequently, I came to see that she was right. I also have come to see that everything actually *is* like safety. The observation that "Every system is perfectly designed to get the results it gets" is the idea that ties safety, equity, and other performance issues together. And problems that are systemic call for systemic solutions.

Tejal had been thinking this way well before the murder of George Floyd. She and coauthor Karthik Sivashanker published an article in *The New England Journal of Medicine* in January 2020 entitled "Advancing Safety and Equity Together."[1] They made the case that there is no such thing as high-quality, safe care that is inequitable, and offered a powerful logic train:

1. There are widespread inequities in health outcomes on the basis of race, sex, and other factors.

2. These inequities have roots in systematic discrimination that has been codified in policies and practices.

3. Our systems are therefore structured to deliver outcomes that vary according to race and other factors.

4. Inequity in healthcare is a systems-based problem that requires a systems-based approach akin to that used to improve patient safety.

Soon thereafter, in an article for *NEJM Catalyst*, Tejal expanded on how lessons learned from patient safety could be applied to DEI.[2] She compared the murder of George Floyd and other recent deaths to the 1999 Institute of Medicine report *To Err Is Human* as galvanizing events that created inflection points. And she described how the four foundational elements for improvement that she and others had described in the National Action Plan for Patient Safety, released in 2020 by the National Steering Committee for Patient Safety, had potential relevance to DEI improvement.[3]

1. **Culture, Leadership, and Governance:** Tejal pointed out how improvement in safety was so often kicked into action by "bold and courageous leaders who were willing to be transparent and to go public about errors at their organizations and what they were doing to improve." The analogous step that has been taken at some (but not all) organizations is sharing data with boards of trustees or directors on differences in patient and employee experiences among groups defined by race, ethnicity, and gender.

2. **Learning Systems:** These systems require infrastructure and senior management (e.g., chief safety officers and chief diversity officers) to have the ability to measure and analyze relevant data, and the effectiveness to develop interventions and track their impact and unintended consequences.

3. **Workforce:** The Safety Report argued that organizations cannot deliver safe care for patients unless the safety of the workforce is protected, too. Similarly, Tejal argued, DEI in the workforce is a precondition to optimal patient experience and quality. (This relationship has subsequently been borne out by extensive analyses at Press Ganey.)

4. **Patient Engagement:** For both safety and equity, building trust begins with transparency. The patient's voice should be prominent in the identification of problems and potential solutions.

The challenges to improving equity are analogous to those that impede progress to zero harm. Leaders need to create an environment of psychological safety in which problems can be identified without fear of repercussion. Data collection systems need to be standardized and improved. And behaviors must be changed and shaped by social norms that make care safer and more equitable.

The big challenge in the comparison of DEI to safety is that it demands that caregivers respond to failures in equity with the same intensity as when they respond to failures in safety. Both are failures. Both are threats to organizational and individual ego identities. Both are painful to acknowledge. And both are even more painful when they recur, so they must be identified and analyzed and plans made to reduce the likelihood of recurrence.

The reality is that inequity *is* a safety problem. It causes physical and emotional harm to both patients and caregivers. For caregivers, it also leads to diminished engagement and resilience, and an increased risk of burnout. For patients, it leads to poorer health outcomes, diminished engagement, and a worse patient experience.

Thinking More Broadly About DEI

DEI is not about any one group of people or about any one problem, and it is not amenable to any one solution. DEI is relevant to the experiences of groups defined by race and ethnicity, but also gender, and physical and intellectual disabilities. To detect any of the four types of harm in these groups requires a measurement and analysis agenda that is both broad and effective. (See Chapter 8.)

The importance of measurement is underscored by data showing how different subgroups of healthcare employees rate their organizations' DEI on a 1 to 5 scale. In every type of job, workers from underrepresented groups give their organizations lower ratings than whites do. Within any racial or ethnic group, managers give the highest average ratings. Other data show that women give lower DEI ratings than men. The implication is that white male managers are likely to have a rosier view of DEI in their organization than their counterparts.

To grasp the full range of issues relevant to DEI for patients, organizations must have a broad approach to measurement. Press Ganey's Equity Partnership was started in July 2020 with a goal of applying an equity lens to all elements of data and data quality. My colleague Deirdre Mylod has defined six key insights relevant to analyzing patient experience scores by race and ethnicity through her coleadership role in that partnership:

1. **Organizations need more than overall measures to understand inequity:** Analyses might *begin* by looking at differences in overall rating or likelihood to recommend, but similar global ratings can mask important differences. For example, the global ratings of hospital care tend to be similar among patients who are Black or African American and those who are Native American or Alaska Native, but the patterns of their responses to specific areas (e.g., how well they were kept informed) are markedly different.

2. **The style of measurement can impact equity findings:** The standard CAHPS patient-experience tools ask patients to report whether something occurred (yes-or-no response) or how often something occurred (never, sometimes, usually, always). Questions with these structures are asking patients about their memory of what happened during their care. Press Ganey measures seek to capture how well things happened by asking respondents to give their evaluations of care on a scale ranging from very poor to very good. In general, our analyses find that

the latter approach demonstrates larger differences in patient experience for non-white patient groups.

3. **Disparities differ by clinical care needs:** This means that organizations need to examine their care separately in different types of settings. Our analyses find that minorities tend to report worse patient experience than whites, but the patterns vary across service lines. Many institutions have considerably lower experience results for minorities in maternity care than for those in medical or surgical service lines, and patterns vary among different racial and ethnic groups.

4. **Disparities differ by care setting:** No one should assume that patterns found for hospitalized patients are relevant to the emergency department or medical practices. The implication is that DEI should be assessed and analyzed for patients with different care needs and in different settings.

5. **Other patient characteristics matter:** In general, surgical patients tend to evaluate their care more favorably than medical patients do. The younger patients are, the less favorably they tend to evaluate care. This holds true up to the age of 80. For patients age 80 and older, the more complex their needs, the lower their ratings. Finally, male patients tend to report better experiences than female patients do. The implication is that all these factors should be taken into account in analyses of DEI patterns.

6. **Identifying inequity in patient experience scores is just the first step of discovery:** The next is asking why the differences occurred, and then developing plans to address the gaps. Racial inequity can and does arise from acts based

in prejudice, but it can also arise from a range of other social, cultural, and behavioral factors affecting patients and caregivers.

Measuring DEI in the Workforce

Measurement of how employees regard the DEI of their work environment has become a critical activity as organizations struggle to improve their cultures and retain employees. My colleagues at Press Ganey designed a five-question "Diversity and Equity Module" that was used only occasionally before 2020, but now we have much more experience with these data. (See Table 9.1.)

Table 9.1 Diversity and Equity Module Scaled Items

Item Text	Domain
This organization values employees from different backgrounds.	Organization
This organization demonstrates a commitment to workplace diversity.	Organization
All employees have an equal opportunity for promotion regardless of their background.	Organization
My coworkers value individuals with different backgrounds.	Employee
The person I report to treats all employees equally regardless of their background.	Manager

The five statements in Table 9.1 provide a high-level view of how their general background affects employees. The organization domain is most prominent in this set of five items because senior leaders need such information to shape organizational culture. The word *background* is used in place of more specific ways in which people might see themselves (e.g., race, ethnicity, religion, gender identity, age, sexual orientation, citizenship status, disability, etc.). To list all such terms in a question would make the survey items too long to hold readers' attention, and leaving any of them out would suggest that equity for that group was not considered important.

These measures are evolving, and Press Ganey has gotten requests to develop and test new measures that go deeper in assessing inclusion. These requests demonstrate the intense interest in improving in DEI, and it will be likely be years before there is anything like a standard set. But I describe them now to encourage readers to be part of the early experience and contribute to developing measures rather than waiting for the standards to emerge. Examples of inclusion pilot items are described in Table 9.2.

Table 9. Pilot Inclusion Items

Item Text	Domain
I can be my authentic self at work.	Employee
This organization has an inclusive culture.	Organization
I feel included in/on my team/work unit.	Employee
Perspectives like mine are included in decision-making.	Organization
I understand my role in maintaining a diverse and inclusive environment.	Employee

There are other optional items that help organizations reliably address employees who identify as lesbian, gay, bisexual, transgender, or queer (LGBTQ), and LGBTQ-specific measures can be included in surveys for organizations seeking more insight into their dynamics of diversity. (See Table 9.3.)

Table 9.3 LGBTQ Scaled Items

Item Text	Domain
This organization protects LGBTQ employees from discriminatory practices.	Organization
This organization does not tolerate bias against LGBTQ employees.	Organization
LGBTQ employees receive the same benefits as everyone else.	Organization
Clinical staff are provided training on LGBTQ patient care.	Organization
Human resources staff are sensitive to LGBTQ workplace concerns.	Organization

The availability of information from these optional DEI survey items has allowed my colleagues to analyze which of the typical workforce engagement items are most strongly correlated with DEI. (See Table 9.4). Our recommendation for organizations seeking to think broadly about DEI is to start by measuring workforce engagement along with the DEI items. When *opportunities for improvement* (AKA *problems*) are identified, consider going deeper with pulse surveys of specific employee subsets, as well as the tools described in the next section.

Table 9.4 Strong Correlates of Diversity and Equity

Item Text	Domain
This organization treats employees with respect.	Organization
I would recommend this organization as a good place to work.	Engagement indicator
Overall, I am a satisfied employee.	Engagement indicator

Item Text	Domain
This organization conducts business in an ethical manner.	Organization
Senior management's actions support this organization's mission and values.	Organization
The actions of the person I report to support this organization's mission and values.	Manager
This organization cares about quality improvement.	Organization
The person I report to cares about quality improvement.	Manager
I have confidence in senior management's leadership.	Organization
The person I report to gives me useful feedback.	Manager
I am proud to tell people I work for this organization.	Engagement indicator
The person I report to encourages teamwork.	Manager
The person I report to values great customer service.	Manager
There is a climate of trust within my work unit.	Employee
The environment at this organization makes employees in my work unit want to go above and beyond what's expected of them.	Employee
This organization makes every effort to deliver safe, error-free care to patients.	Organization
This organization provides high-quality care and service.	Organization

Thinking More Deeply About DEI

As is true for safety, artificial intelligence (AI) and natural language processing (NLP) can be applied to narrative data to get a deeper understanding of what influences DEI from the perspective of patients and employees. My colleagues' work in these areas is just beginning, but the early findings demonstrate the potential value of the insights that result from these analyses. There is a good chance that healthcare organizations will soon want to measure DEI for patients and employees at every unit of the organization, and also apply AI/NLP to the comments returned via surveys.

Senem Guney and Tejal Gandhi described AI-enabled insights into what different racial and ethnic groups of patients say about physicians' courtesy and respect, drawing upon comments from 1.6 million patient experience surveys from January 2020 to September 2021.[4]

They extracted more than 3 million insights from these survey responses and focused on the 683,136 positive and 179,794 negative insights relevant to physician behavior. This remarkable dataset enabled them to explore how drivers of positive experience differed among racial and ethnic groups.

The first important finding was that courtesy and respect was the most prominent theme of positive care experiences with physicians for white, Black, Asian, and Hispanic patients. For each group the theme of courtesy and respect occurred in 20 percent or more of positive insights (20 percent among white and Hispanic patients, 23 percent among Black patients, and 26 percent among Asian patients).

Five subthemes were prominent in all four groups, with modest differences in the distribution—empathy and compassion, kindness, helpfulness, patience, and attentiveness. Hispanic patients described their positive experiences in terms of kindness more often than the other three groups, sometimes emphatically ("[Doctor] showed me a level of kindness I have rarely experienced.")

On the other hand, there was more variation among the four groups' negative insights. For white, Black, and Asian patients, lack of empathy and compassion were the most prominent issues when physicians did not meet their expectations of courtesy and respect. Hispanic patients commented on physicians' rudeness more than any other behavior. White and Hispanic patients mentioned physicians being condescending in 8 to 9 percent of negative insights, but condescension was not among the top five drivers for Black or Asian patients. Asians were the only group that mentioned physicians' lack of patience among their top five negative subthemes.

On the one hand, this analysis showed what common sense would suggest—that people are more alike than different, and that everyone values courtesy and respect. On the other hand, use of AI/NLP to reveal subtle differences among subsets provides a reminder that with every individual patient, caregivers should try to meet their individual needs—for example, by going out of their way to be kind to Hispanic patients and patient with Asian patients. And by making these behaviors into habits, they will hone their instincts for showing courtesy and respect to all their patients.

Leadership Responses

How does an organization get started on the work of pursuing zero inequity? The four basic principles that my colleagues in the Press Ganey Equity Partnership emphasize are:

1. **Using a common language:** Leaders, managers, and all employees should develop a common understanding of equity goals, systematic racism, and unconscious bias.

2. **Having robust data:** This requires knowing which questions to ask and how to understand and analyze the data. It also requires data collection with enough scale to support the necessary data segmentation.

3. **Improving structure and operations:** Effective improvement requires management attention to training,

hiring, retention policies, and procedures that are aligned with equity goals.

4. **Following high-reliability principles:** Organizations need a culture that supports high reliability in pursuing equity as well as safety and other goals.

This work is complex and will never be complete, but it is perhaps the most rewarding work that leaders can undertake. It draws upon the very best of leadership and management skills, including:

- Shaping organizational culture

- Designing reliable and resilient systems

- Balancing system and individual accountability

It also requires the emotional intelligence to recognize the role of cognitive biases, which are often subconscious, and the interpersonal skills to create psychological safety for difficult conversations.

In short, this work may well be what brings the most pride to people working in healthcare, whether they are in senior management or at the front lines of patient care. The following examples from four healthcare organizations, each emphasizing different themes of this work, show what is possible and how zero inequity can be pursued.

Intermountain Healthcare: Starting the Journey

What I like most about Intermountain Healthcare's work on equity is that it arose on the front lines of care but immediately got the strong support of senior management. Denitza Blagev was a young pulmonologist when Covid-19 arrived. In a wonderful *NEJM Catalyst* article, she and her colleagues, including

Intermountain's CEO, Marc Harrison, described how the work began. (Theirs is an article I love because it is written with such honesty and humility.) The authors acknowledge that they are only taking the first steps and that they are going to make missteps. But the journey is underway.[5]

Blagev and coauthors described how two appalling examples of inequity set the work in motion. First, when Covid-19 emerged in Utah in the spring of 2020, she and the other clinicians in the respiratory ICU could not help but notice that nearly half of their patients were Hispanic, Spanish-speaking, and/or non-white. She wrote, "As physicians, we were upset about the inequity. What was not clear was what we could actually do to address it. In May 2020, the murder of George Floyd horrified and shocked us and increased the urgency of our need to act."

Intermountain Healthcare formally adopted equity as one of its values, and started a search for a chief equity officer, a senior medical director of equity and inclusion, and a senior nursing director of equity and inclusion. But, as they wrote, some colleagues expressed skepticism. They quoted one physician as saying, "I don't see why Intermountain is wasting money on a chief equity officer when we don't have a problem with racism." Others wanted to wait until the chief equity officer was recruited and in place before launching any major initiatives.

Blagev and her colleagues did not feel that they could wait months or years to begin this work, however, and decided to model their efforts on other work to improve quality that has earned Intermountain fame over the last few decades. The first step was defining what success would look like. They wanted specific and measurable goals so that they could engage everyone in the work.

They set out to identify key performance indicators, and then create the analytic infrastructure so that managers at every unit of the organization could assess how access and outcomes varied by race, ethnicity, sex, gender, and sexual orientation. They developed equity dashboards that enabled managers to look at trends over time. They also added information on important comorbid conditions so that they could begin to analyze *why* differences in outcomes existed.

The output from these analyses was impressive in its displays but overwhelming in its complexity, so the next step was to use machine-learning algorithms to sort through the information and identify actionable insights. At the same time, they launched major efforts to improve the quality of their data. They knew that their administrative data on race were not reliable, and the result was that they could miss important differences. Working with their not-so-great data on race/ethnicity, they wrote, "If we did find a health disparity, it was likely to be real. If we did not find a disparity, we would have to acknowledge that a disparity may be hidden by the bias of our race and ethnicity data collection."

Intermountain's team reached out to find out how others were addressing this issue and got valuable help from two teams of my own colleagues—one from Mass General Brigham and one from Press Ganey—who were immersed in this work. They decided that the gold standard would be self-reported race/ethnicity data obtained via the electronic Press Ganey surveys. Analyzing that data, they found that white patients were highly likely to be correctly identified as white in administrative data, but that patients of other races were less likely to have their correct race identified in the medical record. As a result, they set up a data-quality team to work on improving data collection on self-reported race/ethnicity.

Meanwhile, they tackled the delicate work of culture change, starting with discomfort and confusion about the use of basic terms such as *gender*, *sex*, *race*, and *ethnicity*, and the meaning of all the letters in LGBTQIA+. "The whole field seemed like a land mine that none of us felt qualified to approach," they wrote.

One analyst said, "We have to be careful if we look at the data, because we don't want people to see any discrepancy and get the wrong idea that we are racist." Blagev responded, quoting a colleague at another institution, "We need to get away from thinking about safe spaces, and instead learn to lean into brave spaces."

The Intermountain team wrote, "We partnered with Press Ganey to address equity in patient experience." This work included analyzing patient experience data disaggregated by race, and—as is true at virtually every institution—they found striking differences. For example, Black or African American patients reported lower patient experience scores in obstetrics compared with other domains, such as medicine and surgery. This particular finding shows the importance of going deep in analyses, and not drawing false comfort from high-level views that mask differences within smaller units of analysis.

"We all have to start somewhere, to begin the work at home, within ourselves, within our organizations, and we need to show concrete steps forward. Even if we stumble and sometimes say the wrong thing, we have to be brave enough to take a thoughtful risk, to listen, and still move forward beyond feeling like it is too big and undefined to yield success," they wrote.

"Our data-driven approach may help engage clinicians and operators in the work. We are aware of and will seek to mitigate the paralysis that may befall some as we face the overwhelming number of inequities. But we believe that to start—and to have measurable outcomes and some success we can build on—will be far better than failing to act while waiting for the one perfect thing to do."

Rush University: Hardwiring a System for Health Equity

An array of impressive initiatives to improve equity are in progress at Rush University Medical Center in Chicago. One, hardwiring equity into the structure of a healthcare system, is ongoing, with new elements being added almost every year. The initiative began in 2016 with the development of the Rush Health Equity Strategy. It included developing means of collaborating with other healthcare organizations and the community to reduce inequity, and also for ensuring that Rush's leadership makes progress toward this goal.

A gating event for the leaders of Rush University Medical Center to begin this work in earnest was the Affordable Care Act, which required that Rush and other not-for-profit hospitals conduct community health needs assessments (CHNA). The findings regarding health gaps were striking. There was a 14-year life expectancy gap and an $84,000 difference in median income between residents of the downtown area and those of the East Garfield Park neighborhood, which was just two train stops away from Rush.

The Rush CHNA report identified structural racism, economic deprivation, and other social and structural determinants of health as the root causes of the dismal life expectancy outcomes so close by. David Ansell and the coauthors of a *NEJM Catalyst* article describing Rush's work on equity wrote, "This CHNA report forced us to ask: What more could we do to address the social and structural determinants of health inside and outside our doors?"[6]

Just as Intermountain Healthcare modeled its initial equity work on successful quality improvement programs, Rush adapted lessons learned from two prior programs that had had a significant impact on racial health inequities. One was a program that had helped reduce the breast cancer mortality disparity between white and Black women in Chicago from 51 percent to 41 percent. The other was a public-private partnership that had improved care for HIV patients. As Ansell wrote, "Both of these programs involved complex partnerships, addressed social determinants of health, tracked health outcome measures, and led with ambitious aims."

Using this model, Rush assembled a team to create a problem statement and secured strong support from the board of trustees. A senior executive was appointed as the strategy leader, reporting to the system CEO and accountable to a subcommittee of the board. In addition, the incentive program for senior executives was modified to create accountability for organizational performance on diversity and equity through an institutional diversity index.

The Rush Equity Framework includes five ambitious pillars of the health equity strategy:

1. **Name and eliminate racism:** Rush leaders emphasized the difference between disparities and inequities. Because the latter are unjust, there is an urgency to correct them.

2. **Adopt an anchor mission:** In January 2017, Rush launched an anchor mission to hire, purchase, invest, and volunteer locally.

3. **Create wealth-building opportunities for employees:** Rush initiated a pension reform program to help employees increase retirement savings, raised entry-level hourly wages to $15, launched healthcare career pathways for employees, and offered financial wellness and credit training.

4. **Eliminate healthcare inequities:** Rush began screening patients for social determinants of health, including food, housing, utility, transportation, and access to primary care.

5. **Address the social and structural determinants of health:** Recognizing that these issues are so large that no organization could take them on alone, Rush worked with other healthcare providers and local community leaders to create West Side United (WSU), a regional health equity collaborative.

When the Covid-19 pandemic hit, WSU was an important part of Chicago's efforts to mitigate its impact on the communities around Rush. Rush intensified its own institutional efforts by convening a multidisciplinary Racial Justice Action Committee to develop a road map for its system. Its five overarching recommendations were:

1. To make racial equity a system strategy

2. To identify a cohort of senior leaders as equity champions

3. To have actionable timelines for change

4. To tie equity outcomes to leaders' performance goals

5. To have an annual system progress report

The first three components of the Rush Health Equity Strategy were the Rush Anchor Mission (2017), the formation of West Side United (2018), and the Racial Justice Action Committee (2020). In 2021, the organization created a fourth component, the Rush Institute for Health Equity, which was supported by a major philanthropic gift. This Institute coordinates the health system's health equity efforts, including educating and training providers, supporting research, and developing new models for practice.

The description of Rush's work ends with this summary:

> The creation of a health equity strategy and realignment of the resources of an academic health system to achieve that strategy, including the formation of a large equity collaborative, carry some unique challenges. However, these changes also provide an opportunity to solve big problems and, therefore, articulate a truly inspirational vision. This, in turn, provides everyone associated with these efforts something of incredible value—hope.

Virginia Mason Medical Center—Building a Culture of Respect

How can healthcare organizations make respect for every patient and every employee a social norm? Virginia Mason Medical Center's Respect for People strategy aims to do just that.

Virginia Mason is famous for its adaptation of the Toyota Production System, known as the Virginia Mason Production System. The VMPS has two core pillars, respect for people and continuous improvement. To strengthen the second pillar, Virginia Mason launched its Respect for People strategy in 2009.[7] It began with a review of relevant organizational data, including culture-of-safety and staff-engagement surveys. The findings highlighted gaps in communication, teamwork, and respect.

In 2010 and 2011, the board of directors adopted Respect for People as a goal, and Virginia Mason developed a list of 10 "foundational behaviors":

1. Be a team player.

2. Listen to understand.

3. Share information.

4. Keep your promises.

5. Speak up.

6. Connect with others.

7. Walk in their shoes.

8. Be encouraging.

9. Express gratitude.

10. Grow and develop.

The program's workshops were presented at off-site performance spaces, and Virginia Mason leaders led discussions afterward. A wide variety of unconventional tools were used to make the 10 behaviors recognizable as goals. For example, an acting troupe performed vignettes capturing disrespectful interactions based on actual experiences across a broad spectrum of job categories. More than 99 percent of employees, including physicians and board members, attended a workshop.

In keeping with Virginia Mason's other pillar, continuous improvement, all the participants were asked to commit to personal development on two behaviors. In work units, posters showed team members discussing their selected behaviors. A range of other steps were taken to nudge along the cultural transformation. There was statistically significant improvement on measures of safety culture, such was whether staff felt free to speak up and question the actions of those with more authority.

But the initial improvement was not sustained, and Virginia Mason decided to refresh its program in 2016. In this next phase, Virginia Mason sought to heighten employees' sensibilities about how it feels to experience disrespect. They broadened the definitions of the foundational behaviors to reflect the need to improve diversity, equity, and inclusion. They ran town halls to discuss the challenges, collected new data, and enlisted an acting troupe to produce a 90-minute summit that was performed for more than 5,400 of Virginia Mason's team members. The participation rate was 94 percent.

This time, the scenarios and large group discussions directly addressed DEI issues including microaffirmations, microaggressions, and unconscious bias. They portrayed *upstanding* (standing up for someone who is being disrespected) and *bystanding* (observing a disrespectful interaction but not taking action against it). Videos showed one Code Blue with disrespectful behavior and another with respectful behavior. Leaders conducted discussions about diversity, inclusion, speaking up, and psychological safety.

When the impact of the Respect for People program was assessed, surveys of employees showed statistically significant improvement on the following questions framed as statements, with respondents asked to express levels of agreement on a six-choice scale:

- I adjust the way I speak and interact in order to be respectful to everyone.

- I know how to share feedback with others when I see or experience disrespect.

- I say thanks as soon as possible in response to respectful behavior.

- The members of my work team value and respect each other's contributions.

The percentage of respondents who indicated that they knew how to share feedback when witnessing or experiencing disrespect rose from 45 percent to 63 percent (P<0.001). Although it is impossible to identify cause and effect with precision, Virginia Mason also saw steady improvement on patient experience surveys on questions about whether patients felt they were treated with respect by physicians and nurses.

The challenge, Virginia Mason leaders know, is sustaining improvement. They have given careful thought to the nature of the work of changing culture, and they clearly know that they will never stop learning, and that there is likely to be backsliding on their progress if they lapse into complacency. That mindset is completely consistent with the nature of the Virginia Mason Production System.

Parkland Health & Hospital System (PHHS): Integrating Public Health and Healthcare Delivery

Parkland, the safety-net health system for Dallas, has worked closely and creatively with Dallas County Health and Human Services (DCHHS) throughout the Covid-19 pandemic. Their efforts and initiatives are likely to be sustained after the pandemic has eased, and they should be considered for emulation elsewhere.[8]

In 2019, PHHS and DCHHS worked together to complete a CHNA like the one performed by Rush University, and the findings were similar. For example, the life expectancy in south Dallas zip code 75215 was 23 years less than that in the more affluent 75204 area. But what to do about it?

To better understand the drivers of the differences, PHHS helped start an affiliated organization called the Parkland Center for Clinical Innovation (PCCI), which collects and analyzes a wide variety of data, including information on income, education, employment, and housing status. It has developed a Social Needs Index (SNI) that correlates well with poorer health outcomes and helps identify areas of the county with the greatest need for interventions.

Even before the Covid-19 pandemic, PHHS and DCHHS were using this information to develop and implement a multi-pronged plan to address the root causes of inequities. This plan focused on zip codes with high SNI, and supported a wide range of interventions, including support from social services and improved access to healthy food, physical activity, and tobacco-free environments. The interventions ranged well beyond programs closely related to healthcare; for example, they included targeted employee recruitment, hiring and career development, and community investment via local vendors—some of the same areas Rush University's equity work chose to focus on.

When the pandemic arrived, the leaders of Parkland and DCHHS met to create a regional approach to Covid-19 testing and located sites in high SNI areas that commercial testing sites would be likely to miss. The two sites each tested 1,000 individuals per day. Of the recipients of the 150,000 tests performed in March–December 2020, 30 percent self-identified as Black and 49 percent self-identified as Hispanic/Latino. Parkland also began testing inmates in the Dallas County jail, where the test positivity rate was over 20 percent. Among inmates in juvenile detention centers, the positivity rate was 30 percent.

PHHS, PCCI, and DCHHS collaborated to identify people most at risk of exposure, alert them to risk, and provide early diagnosis and treatment for people already infected. This solution used public health Covid-19 case reports for geographic information system mapping. A machine-learning algorithm with geo-mapping and hot-spotting technology generated a Proximity Index (PI)—a personal risk score based on individuals' proximity to confirmed, active Covid-19 cases. PCCI created a Vulnerability Index (VI) that analyzed individual mobility using publicly available cell phone app data and the location of new Covid-19 cases and was thus able to help identify high-risk areas of emerging disease.

The data from these analyses were used to identify patients at high risk who had an upcoming clinic appointment, allowing nurses to reach out and assess whether the patient should be tested before the appointment or whether the appointment should be converted to a virtual visit. In the first year, 16 percent of patients identified as high risk and triaged reported Covid-19-like symptoms, and 25 percent reported potential exposure.

As the pandemic eases, this collaboration—involving data sharing and integration among the healthcare delivery and public health systems—seems likely to endure. Parkland leaders note that the provider and public health organizations have always worked together informally, but "while this loose integration may be sufficient when not under stress, the pandemic has demonstrated the need for a deeper level of integration between the delivery system and the public health system. To be maximally effective, this integration must be developed and functional before the onset of a crisis."

We still have much to do to pursue the goal of zero inequity, but it is great work. It involves shaping the internal culture of healthcare organizations, as at Virginia Mason, and collaborating with outside organizations in pursuit of noble shared goals, as at Parkland. It requires changing the structure of organizations, as at Rush, and embarking on data-driven improvement, as at Intermountain.

The incentives are compelling. And the methods for measuring and improving are increasingly clear.

Consumerism

THERE MAY STILL be leaders of healthcare organizations who look down their noses at consumerism. They think of it as a necessary evil and something to dismiss in order to focus on things that matter more. The time has arrived for those leaders to reassess their perspective.

They should instead understand that consumerism is enduring and important, and it poses an opportunity to build patients' trust. Demographic and technology shifts have transformed the way people interact with everything, including their healthcare. People know that they have choices. They know they can access information. They want to get their needs met quickly, conveniently, and affordably—and they know that if they shop around, they just might get what they want.

The right move for healthcare organizations is to embrace consumerism. Think of it as a logical extension of patient-centered care. It is organizing around meeting patients' needs, with a broadened concept of the needs that matter, including the need for information. Consumerism can also make it easier for healthcare organizations to meet patients' needs rather than being indifferent or inattentive to how they are met beyond face-to-face interactions with clinicians.

It means looking for friction in the processes through which people get their healthcare needs met, and relentlessly working to reduce it. Where there is friction, there is opportunity to improve—even if the friction lies outside the traditional walls of the organization. Where there is friction, there is also an opportunity to enhance the trust of patients and the pride of employees.

What People Want

Most healthcare leaders have a visceral sense of what modern consumers want—after all, they have plenty of practice being consumers themselves. Healthcare consumers want ease and convenience, of course, but they also want their needs to be met really well. They want information when they ask a question, and when they need deeper interactions, they want them to happen quickly and conveniently.

That said, what people want is nuanced, and when colleagues pointed that out to me, I experienced minor revelations. Despite the risk of embarrassment, I will share them. First, when patients experience friction early in their episode, it colors how they perceive the entire episode. In other words, that early period, before patients even start to interact with the healthcare system, matters.

It is clearly important to make sure processes work smoothly once patients call or log onto providers' websites. But it may also be important to go further upstream and consider what they are seeing on the internet when they first begin their research. The chance to build or erode trust begins that early.

Another modest revelation for me has been the importance of replying to patient feedback in the public sphere. Upon facing criticism of my organization or myself in a patient comment, my natural reaction has been to ignore it. I don't like calling attention to the criticism, and, perhaps subconsciously, I tend to pretend it didn't happen.

A better reaction may be to actually respond. I cannot cite data to support this observation, but my colleagues believe that when you do service recovery on a one-to-one basis with a patient on the phone, multiple good things can happen. Having that conversation makes explicit the team's intention to make the patient feel heard. It humanizes the institution. Moreover, there is always the chance of learning more about how to address the issue.

My colleagues believe that replying to a Google or Health-grades review has those same benefits, with the added aspect that it lives online for future patients to see. It provides a nearly unlimited opportunity to show that the institution is listening to patients and humanize the brand to the public. Responding to online reviews can address issues before they arise, since future patients can use the information they learn.

A third epiphany is that patients *really* are not thinking about discrete transactions (e.g., how did the visit go?), but are thinking much more in terms of the long-term relationships. And in these relationships, they are not actually expecting their caregivers to be perfect.

It's very inconvenient, and just plain painful, for a patient to change doctors once they establish a relationship. They are looking for the right blend of downsides and upsides that match their own priorities. For example, many patients love one of my colleagues, who always runs terribly late. Once people are in the room with him, he gives them his full attention and takes as much time as needed with each of them. They may sit in the waiting room for an hour or more beyond their scheduled appointment time, but they know what they are getting, and they feel lucky to have him as their doctor. However, there are other patients who would be outraged to be kept waiting for more than a few minutes.

This observation means that doctors don't need to be perfect; they just need to be consistent. And part of the goal of providing information such as ratings and comments is to show consumers the good sides and the minor flaws, and let the patient decide what doctor is the best fit for them. Our experts in this area believe that patients tend to make their choices on the basis of the positives that are highlighted, not the negatives. They don't seem to hold one or two negative comments against clinicians—in fact, if all comments are euphoric, it calls into question the authenticity of the data.

Once patients make a choice, they are more likely to feel good about their overall care. Their thinking is, "I choose you knowing your flaws, so I am much more willing to accept and minimize them, because to do otherwise would mean that I was wrong in my choice."

A fourth revelation is that patient reviews tend to get read more than the blurbs that organizations offer about physicians—and for a good reason; those blurbs are written for the physician. They usually do not address the issues that are most important to patients, such as how it is going to feel to have this doctor take care of them. Doctors don't need to share details about their hobbies and interests (like marketing leaders might claim). Instead, they need to share their philosophy of care, how they deliver the best medicine, how they keep their patients safe, and how they work with their teams. Our experts find that when physicians make an effort to make and share videos (emphasizing authenticity, not airbrushed production perfection), consumers watch them, spend time trying to get to know their doctors, and read reviews.

At an organizational level (rather than that of the individual clinician), there are some more subtle needs that can differentiate organizations from their competitors. One is consistency, so that patients don't have to rediscover how to navigate systems over and over and over. This consistency should characterize physical systems (e.g., facility signage and layouts) and information systems (e.g., all the orthopedists in a system have web pages with the same appearance and content so that comparisons can be made without frustration).

Another thing patients appreciate is improvement itself. They love the moment when something that was clunky in the past can be done easily. When processes surrounding care (e.g., reaching a practice to make an appointment) improve, it suggests that other things in the organization are probably changing for the better, too. This helps earn the trust of patients.

My colleagues at Press Ganey did an extensive consumerism survey in 2021. The findings underscore how the patient experience can no longer be defined by what happens exclusively in the clinical setting. Granted, the survey respondents were all internet users, so the data may reflect the leading edge more than the current mainstream of patients, but the trends are obvious. Today, patient experience involves the entire healthcare journey, including internet searches, scheduling, virtual visits, and billing.

The key takeaways:

- **Digital drives choice:** Patients rely on digital resources 2.2 times more than provider referrals when choosing a healthcare provider.

- **Consumers use digital a lot:** Consumers used an average of three different websites during their healthcare research process and read 5.5 reviews before making a decision.

- **Patients are discerning:** Eighty-four percent of respondents indicated that they would not pick a referred provider with a rating below four stars.

- **Online scheduling is preferred:** Most patients (63 percent) preferred to book appointments digitally, while only 37 percent preferred to use the phone.

- **Patients know they are customers:** Assuming no concerns about quality of care, patients rated customer service (71 percent) and communication (63 percent) as more important than even bedside manner.

- **Virtual health is a growing trend:** Over one-third of patients had used telehealth in the past year.

The implications for leaders of healthcare organizations are clear, disruptive, and even painful. The top five factors that emerged when survey respondents were asked what impacted their decisions to choose one healthcare provider over another were:

1. Positive online reputation, indicated by four stars or more (59 percent)

2. Relevant and accurate information online (58 percent)

3. Ability to schedule or reschedule appointments online (48 percent)

4. Availability of reviews on healthcare review sites (40 percent)

5. Ability to private message a healthcare provider (25 percent)

These findings mean providers must take on something that has traditionally seemed beyond their control (i.e., how they appear on the internet) and work to remove friction from the process of getting access to care, even if it means persuading their physicians to give up their traditional control over how appointments are made. This also requires standardizing such processes so that patients get a consistent experience as they seek care, make appointments, and receive follow-up information.

The reason to do such work is deeper than surrendering to the power of consumers and giving them what they want. The underlying reason is to build trust among patients—the sense that they can depend on the providers to take care of them no matter what happens. This is also the ultimate goal of consumers, and why they want web interfaces that are rich in information, consistent, and easy to use.

Patients don't want to pick a physician or a facility with mixed reviews. They want to pick providers with consistent four- or five-star ratings on the multiple sites that they visit. And they want those sites to be rich with data—the more the better. Who wants to buy a book that has only two reviews on Amazon? Similarly, who wants to pick a physician for whom the only information available is where they underwent training?

The Press Ganey survey showed that reviews were the single most important factor in a patient's decision to book an appointment with a provider, but not all reviews were created equal. Patients valued authentic and informative reviews more than the total volume. Most patients (61 percent) indicated that reviews of poor quality would actually discourage them from choosing a provider. They also want recent reviews, because they believe (logically) that more recent reviews provide insight into the current care of the practice.

Beyond scrutinizing the reviews, survey respondents valued convenience factors, like communication, appointment booking, and a seamless intake/registration process. When they were asked to describe important factors beyond receiving excellent care, the top issues that emerged were:

- Quality of customer service (71 percent)

- Cleanliness of facilities (68 percent)

- Communication (e.g., follow-up appointment reminders, annual checkup reminders) (63 percent)

- Bedside manner of the provider (63 percent)

- Ease of appointment booking (59 percent)

- Quality and accuracy of information (40 percent)

- Availability of telehealth services (22 percent)

- Waiting room amenities (22 percent)

Respondents listed the following as factors that would discourage them from booking an appointment with a provider:

- Difficulty contacting the office (e.g., long hold times) (62 percent)

- Poor quality or reviews (e.g., reviews seem sponsored and/ or untrustworthy) (61 percent)

- Average rating of less than four stars (39 percent)

- Incomplete listing information (e.g., not enough relevant information found online) (37 percent)

- Outdated, hard-to-navigate website (35 percent)

- Incomplete doctor profile on hospital or third-party directory (e.g., no headshot, biographical information) (32 percent)

- Lack of online scheduling options (29 percent)

- Not enough patient reviews on third-party websites (25 percent)

- Lack of telehealth options (18 percent)

Patients cared about getting good and helpful information before and after visits. More than a third indicated that they appreciated getting text and email appointment reminders. These preferences were influenced by age/generation. Forty-four percent of baby boomers preferred to use their smartphones and tablets to research healthcare providers; 39 percent wanted to schedule their visits online. The percentages were higher for younger patients.

In short, the process of building trust begins by giving consumers/patients the information they want right from the start and in a format that feels familiar because it is consistent across the organization. The process continues when organizations have made it easy to act on the information. Press Ganey survey data indicate that respondents of all ages are not happy with how systems currently work. This means there is enormous opportunity for organizations that can most effectively improve the consumer experience.

Managing the Flow of Information

Healthcare organizations know there is a ton of information about them online, but they have not tried to manage it. The sources include insurance companies, government organizations, advocacy groups, and providers themselves. The data flow through a range of search engines (e.g., Google and Bing), social media companies (e.g., Meta/Facebook), and third-party reporting sites (e.g., Healthgrades and Vitals). Much of the information is out of date or just plain wrong. Many online "reviews" from "patients" are not authentic, and some physician reviews may have been written by someone who never actually saw the clinician. What emerges during patients' web searches is more a matter of chance than either patients or healthcare organizations would like.

Rather than just let their reputations on the web just happen, healthcare organizations should take on the work of managing their reputations—in part to protect their brands, but also to build the trust of patients and make their experiences smoother. The leaders should swallow hard and repeat this phrase as their mantra: *Transparency is good.* The more data that are shared, the better. And if the data are shared widely, better still.

The implication is that healthcare organizations should not only share their data, but they should also push it beyond their organizational walls. The data will be more accurate than comments that have been posted online, and thus more likely to paint a favorable picture of the organization because people who take the time to spontaneously offer comments are more likely to be unhappy than the overall patient population. By being more transparent and pushing more representative data farther out on the web, providers will improve the accuracy and the consistency of what patients find, while burnishing their brand.

The first step in managing the flow of information is to think in a structured way about the types of information that are or could be made available. The list includes:

1. Performance metrics (e.g., HEDIS measures)

2. Basic provider data

3. More advanced provider data (e.g., videos)

4. Patient ratings and comments

5. Appointment availability

The second step is to think about the types of interfaces patients can access, and have processes for working with each of them. The list includes:

1. Search engines, maps, social, and local sites (e.g., Google, Bing, Twitter, Facebook, Waze, Apple Maps)

2. Provider organization sites

3. Consumer healthcare directories (e.g., Healthgrades, WebMD, Vitals, and Wellness.com)

4. Health insurers (e.g., UnitedHealthcare, Aetna, Blue Cross Blue Shield, and the payer-side of payer-provider organizations such as Providence Health Plan and Geisinger Health Plan)

5. Pharma brand sites (e.g., Novartis, AbbVie)

6. Government databases (e.g., Medicare.gov)

Organizations should decide which data and functions they are ready to implement on their own sites and how extensively they will work with external sites. The more data and functions that they are willing to provide on their own sites, the better, and providing data and making functions available on other sites extends the organization's reach.

Where the Puck Is Going

As a general rule, I don't like to use sports analogies, but sometimes they are just perfect. The one that seems most relevant to consumerism in healthcare is the famous quote from the father of hockey great Wayne Gretzky, who told his son not to skate to where the puck was, but to go to where the puck was going to be.

For healthcare organizations, it seems clear where the puck is going. Transparency is one destination, consistency is another, and reducing friction is a third.

It seems highly likely that most organizations will provide data like patient ratings and comments to external sites in the near future. And it seems likely that well-organized delivery systems will create web presences that have accurate data, clean and consistent appearances, and easy-to-use functionality. It will be surprising if most healthcare organizations have not enabled digital appointment making on their own sites within a few years, and are not extending that function to other sites.

The organizations that move in these directions fastest will have a distinct competitive advantage over their peers.

CHAPTER 11

The New Marketplace

THERE ARE PEOPLE working in provider organizations who view health insurance plans as enemies, asserting that their main activity is to look for excuses to deny payments. The converse is also true. There are people working at health insurance plans who see provider organizations as the source of society's healthcare cost problems, asserting that providers are relentlessly trying to wring as much revenue as possible out of the fee-for-service system.

Whatever kernels of truth exist in these negative assessments, the years ahead demand that providers and payers find ways to collaborate to improve the experience and the value of patient care. Both payers and providers have increasingly compelling business incentives to improve on both fronts, and they can be much more successful if they work together than if they do not.

In this chapter, I won't try to cover all aspects of the evolving healthcare marketplace but will focus on the reasons for payers and providers to collaborate and offer some examples and recommendations for win-win-win strategic initiatives. (Patients would also be winners.) I'll focus first on the reasons to collaborate on improving member/patient experience, and then turn to the overarching goal of increasing the value of healthcare with examples of collaborative improvement models, including descriptions of potential focuses for collaboration of payers, providers, and payer-providers.

Working Together to Improve Member/Patient Experience

No one really wants healthcare to be just about money, but whenever money is involved, it tends to draw attention away from nearly everything else. For this reason, it's a sign of progress that financial incentives are increasingly being used to promote something other than the volume of services performed—as part of contracts between the government and insurance plans, and between insurance plans and healthcare providers. Although there is no perfect way to get financial incentives for quality exactly right, any reward for quality does more good than harm. In fact, it doesn't take much money to get organizations or clinicians behind doing something that they know is a good thing: a small incentive can be just the nudge that is needed.

The big change in incentives for health insurance plans in the last couple of years is the growing emphasis on how members of their health plans rate their experience when they are contacted for surveys. For example, the Center for Medicare and Medicaid Services (CMS) has shifted the focus for its quality incentives for Medicare Advantage plans from gap closure (e.g., ensuring that preventive tests such as mammograms are performed) to improvement of member experience. The United States is about to cross the point at which a majority of Americans who are insured by Medicare

are covered by Medicare Advantage plans, and this shift means that substantial proportions of government payments to health plans will be determined by member-experience survey results.

Suddenly, health plans that have measured member experience—mostly motivated by the need to comply with regulatory requirements—are facing the reality that they must also figure out how to improve it. And when they look at the key drivers of member experience, they immediately see that it will be difficult to improve without working with providers.

Press Ganey's subsidiary, SPH Analytics, has analyzed the key drivers of overall member experience with health plans. Virtually all of the top 20 drivers of member experience are completely or largely under the influence of healthcare providers, including:

1. Healthcare quality overall

2. Personal and specialist physician quality

3. Doctors listening carefully

4. Getting urgent care

5. Doctors showing respect

6. Getting care/tests/treatment

7. Getting routine care

8. Doctors providing clear explanations

9. Doctors spending enough time

10. Getting a specialist appointment

11. Doctors discussing medications

12. Being seen within 15 minutes of appointment

13. Doctors informing about care

14. Doctors having medical records/information

15. Getting test results

16. Getting help managing care

Clearly, the best single strategy that health insurance plans have for improving their member experience is to encourage their healthcare providers to deliver care that is accessible, empathic, well-communicated, and just plain better.

Healthcare providers have every incentive to improve patient experience—even those aspects that aren't under their direct control. For example, when I prescribe a medication that is not covered by the insurer and the patient cannot pick it up from the drugstore, that patient may not blame me, but the friction does not reflect well on me, either. We've learned that there is widespread spillover in patient experience; unwanted experiences in any aspect of care taint everyone.

When compared to patients admitted electively to a given hospital floor, those admitted from the emergency department to the same floor tend to give lower ratings to the care they receive there. Similarly, patients who do not go directly home but instead are discharged to a skilled nursing facility give their hospital care lower ratings, too. Our best understanding is that the unpleasant experiences of emergency and nonacute care color their recollection of what happened on the floors of the hospital. No one has done a randomized controlled trial, but it is logical to assume that chaos in any part of a patient's care taints their ratings of everyone involved.

Here's an example from my own practice that nearly drove me crazy a few years ago: One of my patients with diabetes needed to begin taking insulin because her glucose control on oral medications was terrible. The problem was that she was in the donut hole of her Medicare supplement's drug coverage, so she would have to pay hundreds of dollars a month for insulin—a drug that was nearly a century old. She told me that she just couldn't afford it and asked me to find a less expensive way to treat her diabetes.

I spent many hours talking to colleagues and pharmacists, looking for a way to get her access to lower-cost insulin. It just wasn't possible. I might have felt good about myself for trying harder than many physicians would have tried but, essentially, I had failed. And that was the way it looked to my patient, too.

I cite this example to make the point that the best resolution would not have been for the insurance company to adopt a policy of covering anything I order. There are reasons, after all, that health insurance plans have to put the brakes on spending. Someone has to say no in some instances, and physicians do not particularly like taking on that role. The best resolution may be for the insurance company to work with providers like me to meet patients' needs. That is possible, as some of the following examples will show.

Working Together to Improve the Value of Care

We need to ensure that all people have high-quality care at a cost that society can afford. The goal of universal access to good care is widely considered a right, but for every right that a society creates, it must assign someone the responsibility of ensuring that that right is protected. That responsibility falls collectively on government, health insurers, and healthcare providers. None of them alone can guarantee a patient's right to good care; it takes all of them working together.

To shift from an idealistic to a practical perspective, it is also very much in the interests of all three groups to work toward affordable universal coverage of high-quality care. For government, that goal helps reduce inequity. For providers, it reduces the angst and dysfunction associated with trying to take care of patients who are uninsured or underinsured (like my patient who could not afford her prescribed insulin). For health insurance plans, it offers the chance to move from brokering the flow of money to brokering the creation of value, which may be more difficult but can be more durable as a strategy.

For these reasons, the growth of Medicare Advantage, to the extent that most Americans on Medicare will be covered by managed-care plans, can be seen as an important inflection point in the movement away from pure fee-for-service and toward value-based care. The same trend is underway with Medicaid. And both forms of government-based insurance are growing while employer-based insurance is shrinking. The bottom line is that health plans and providers are recognizing that working within managed Medicare and Medicaid products is a huge part of their future.

Thriving under these products is actually feasible, and completely consistent with the values and goals asserted in this book. It takes building trust with patients, teamwork, good communication, and high reliability in all the major types of performance. This work is completely aligned with improving member and patient experience. Accordingly, the strategic move for healthcare organizations is to plunge into the shift toward value-based care and build the payer-provider relationship and other collaborations necessary to succeed.

Forming Productive Collaborations

What does collaboration between a payer and a provider look like? I love the following example from a delivery system that has both insurance and provider functions. (Because, as I finish this manuscript, the health plan has not yet extended the same approach to physicians who are not employed by the organization, it asks that I not use its name.)

All the cancer clinicians in the health system agreed to adhere to specific protocols for diagnosis and treatment of common cancers. This established trust that the system's clinicians would not be using tests and treatments differently from the guidelines, so the health plan no longer required the clinicians to get prior authorization for tests and treatments. As a result, the clinicians could immediately make plans and start treatments for patients with newly diagnosed cancers. There were no more administrative delays. The days from diagnosis to developing a plan went from one week to one day.

I doubt that this development will change clinical outcomes much, if at all, but I am sure that it will save patients several sleepless nights as they wait for their treatments to begin. It has also reduced costs and aggravation for both the health plan and the clinicians. But that didn't just happen because the health plan surrendered to the clinicians and got rid of its prior authorization program. It happened because the clinicians were ready to create social capital by agreeing to adhere to protocols, thus winning the trust of the health plan by ensuring that resources would not be wasted on low-value care.

Another type of collaboration uses artificial intelligence (AI) to reduce the friction of payment-related interactions faced by both the payers and providers. Some providers use AI to up-code diagnoses to maximize reimbursement, and some payers use AI to identify claims to deny. But there are also uses of AI on both sides aimed at speeding interactions, improving reliability, and reducing the extent to which patients are held hostage by payer-provider tussles over money.

For example, providers are using AI to identify claims that are at high risk for being denied by payers, so they can address the issues before they submit the claims. Payers are using AI to identify requests for high-cost tests and treatments that are likely to be approved—and then just approving them. There are still arguments to be made for and against this type of automation, but AI is making it possible to get rid of many interactions that are a waste of employee time on both sides.

Using AI to improve interactions between payers and providers works better when they collaborate. And, once again, patients benefit by having less chaos in their care.

Areas of Focus for Payers, Providers, and Payer-Providers

Collaboration is a compelling path toward addressing issues that are important to all parties, particularly increasing transparency, access, and quality, and reducing costs.

Transparency satisfies patients' desire for information so that they can make choices or have more trust in their decisions. Providers should not only furnish information on their own websites, but also actively push it out to third-party sites to build patients' trust. Providers and payers can collaborate in the new marketplace by letting payers include information on providers on their websites. Payers would be well-advised to give providers an incentive to be transparent rather than try to negotiate specific quality-improvement targets and tie money to them.

Access is ripe for collaboration because both payers and providers want to improve it. There are many complex steps that can be taken to improve access, but there is also a simple one—moving to digital appointment access. Patients should be able to make their appointments via the internet, without having to talk to a human being. They should also be able to do this from third-party sites—especially payer websites that serve as provider directories.

Quality is a term that can be so vague it eludes defining specific goals for improvement. But a simple goal, for which all interests are aligned, is reducing friction for patients anywhere in the care process. Working together to identify friction points and working together to eliminate them serves all interests. An example is collaborating to help smooth patient transportation issues—an area in which neither payer nor provider takes responsibility but which greatly influences the extent to which patients experience chaos in their care.

The fourth and final area is collaborating to control healthcare costs. This means more than trying to be efficient. It means trying to reduce overall healthcare spending so that resources are available to address the social issues that are such powerful determinants of health. For this reason, providers should be ready to plunge into contracts that reward them for value (e.g., ACO contracts), and payers should be ready to work with them to make those contracts viable on a long-term basis.

The Covid-19 years have shown what is possible when payers and providers work together on an important problem. It was the right thing to do for public health and the right thing to do for patients. Collaboration toward those same goals will provide a strategic advantage for healthcare organizations in the years ahead.

CHAPTER 12

New Skills for the Era Ahead

HEALTHCARE ORGANIZATIONS TODAY need to perform as systems, and that includes responding as a system to challenges that emerge from prolonged crises, such as a pandemic or from the need for social change. The ability to respond quickly to turmoil represents a departure from the past, when the relatively slow evolution of the marketplace rewarded an incremental approach to change. But this imperative has been made explicit by the three perfect storms of recent years: the health storm produced by the Covid-19 pandemic; the economic storm that resulted from the closure of the economy; and the social storm that followed the murder of George Floyd in May 2020, which sparked fresh outrage at longstanding social inequities.

Even as leaders weathered these storms, they and their organizations were adapting to new realities. During a year in which so many interactions were conducted virtually, the digital sophistication of many people increased enormously. This change has encouraged patients to behave more like consumers than they have in the past. In response, healthcare organizations are realizing that patient experience really commences when people begin their web searches.

Meanwhile, society and the healthcare marketplace has continued to evolve in ways that create new pressures for performance. Two major trends are the aging of the baby boomers and the growing prevalence of managed Medicare and Medicaid insurance products for patients and healthcare providers.

Another reality is the likelihood that uncertainty itself is here to stay. In this context, healthcare organizations must develop new levels of resilience—not only maintaining morale during difficult times, but also adapting in the face of the unexpected and redesigning care on the fly. As they manage their challenges, they must retain the trust of consumers, of patients, and of their workforce. All of these people are unsettled by disruptions and deeply concerned about their safety and whether their needs are being heard.

Managing these challenges means more than avoiding missteps. To thrive, healthcare organizations must pursue goals that might have been taken for granted or considered to be narrower in scope in the past. As framed in this book, these goals include:

1. Deserve, earn, and build trust of patients (Chapter 6).

2. Deserve, earn, and build trust of the healthcare workforce (Chapter 7).

3. Build a high-reliability culture with a broadened concept of safety (Chapter 8).

4. Build an inclusive culture that treats every patient and every employee with respect (Chapter 9).

5. Extend patient-centeredness to embrace consumerism, and work relentlessly to remove friction from the experience of consumers/patients (Chapter 10).

6. Respond to the imperatives of the new marketplace for high-value care characterized by a smooth member/patient experience (Chapter 11).

In many organizations, these issues are owned by different senior managers. For example, chief human resources officers may be responsible for improving engagement. Safety culture may be the focus for chief safety officers. Equity may be the focus for chief diversity officers. Clearly, work to improve all these important focuses should be integrated and taken on together.

However, there are specific skills that are crucial for people working at different levels of the organization. This final chapter will describe three critical skills for each of three overlapping types of people working in healthcare: (1) leaders (including boards), (2) managers (from senior executives to managers directly responsible for patient care), and (3) clinicians and other employees working at the front lines of care.

Leaders and Boards

Leadership at the top of healthcare organizations must master three skills: articulating the core values of the organization, developing strategy, and understanding the value chain of activities necessary to execute that strategy.

That first skill—articulating core values—is essential for earning the trust of patients and employees. To paraphrase Ralph Waldo Emerson, every institution is the lengthened shadow of its leadership. This concept is reflected in Frances Frei's model for trust. Leaders must show that they understand what is important to patients and their employees, and that they are authentic in embracing the values that resonate with them.

In articulating those values, I like the advice former Aetna CEO Ron Williams gave in the interview I did with him in 2021 for *NEJM Catalyst*. He said, "If you say that you're a values-based organization and you do not start every opportunity to speak to employees, to speak to customers, to speak to clients, to speak to the board, with the values of that organization, then the values are implicitly unimportant. Your own behavior in meetings, in events, has to be extremely consistent with authentic behavior.

"Your culture is what a new employee experiences after they've been to orientation, they've seen a video, they've heard you speak, and they go to lunch when they meet with one of their buddies," he continued. "They lean over the table and they say, 'Now tell me how it really works around here.' What that employee says is the culture of the organization. Your job through the authentic communication, consistency and repetition, and demonstrated behavior is to align what that employee experiences and articulates with what you want the culture to be."

The second skill, developing strategy, is critical during times of turmoil because, as explained by my colleague Michael Porter, that is when it is most important to have a laser-like focus on the questions at the core of strategy. Organizations must have a clear idea of who their key customer is, and of the value they create for that customer. In healthcare, that means reducing the suffering of patients. Organizations can never lose sight of that fundamental goal, and it should determine their choices about what to do and what not to do.

The third skill, understanding the chain of activities needed to create value—helps focus leaders and boards on what they should be doing. Among those activities is meeting the needs of the workforce and building trust and engagement among employees. These activities include ensuring safety (with an expanded concept that includes emotional and financial harm) for patients and employees, and making real progress on diversity, equity, and inclusion.

A key lesson of the last few years is that organizations cannot control all the activities that are essential elements of the value chain and must be ready to collaborate with other organizations to optimize performance. As described in Chapter 11, providers that are ready to work closely with payers have the potential to meet patients' needs better than their competitors. And providers should be ready to work with outside organizations to reduce friction for consumers. These opportunities mean that managing interdependencies should be considered a priority on the same level as management within the walls of the organization.

Managers

Three essential skills for managers at all levels of the organization are creating social capital, implementing high-reliability principles, and eliminating waste of all types.

As noted earlier in the book, financial capital refers to the monetary resources that allow organizations to do things they otherwise couldn't do. Human capital refers to the people that allow organizations to do things they otherwise couldn't do. Social capital describes how those people interact with each other and with the surrounding infrastructure so the organization can do things it otherwise couldn't do.

Managers create the social capital of the organization, which is more precious than financial capital, since money can be borrowed from banks. Managers can set the tone of the workplace, ensure a culture of trust and respect, and create a growth mindset. The managers in the C-suite are important, but the managers close to the front lines of care are the ones who shape the microcultures in which people work.

Managers also bring the principles of high-reliability organizations to life. They must despise errors of all types and with such passion that they are always primed to recognize when mistakes have occurred. Then, they must be able to identify the errors, study them, learn from them, and do what it takes to reduce the chances that they will happen again. Managers are the ones who generate data and use them to improve.

Managers should also work relentlessly to eliminate waste—wasted resources that increase costs and wasted time for patients and employees that causes annoyance and dysfunction in patient care. Eliminating waste also means fighting the waste of people—e.g., the duress and burnout that cause so many to leave healthcare, and the inequity and lack of inclusion that compromise cultures in so many organizations.

Frontline Caregivers

Three essential skills for frontline caregivers—including clinicians and those who are not directly involved in patient care—are creating a culture of respect, fully participating in great teams, and shaping the stories and memories of patients.

The first skill, creating a culture of respect, is an essential part of making healthcare organizations that seek to become as inclusive and equitable as they should be. The objective that is analogous to the safety goal of zero harm is that every patient and every caregiver should feel that they are respected, that they are believed, and that their problems matter. Any deviation from that admittedly idealistic goal seems hard to justify. It is clearly possible in smaller groups, and there is no reason why it cannot become the compelling social norm throughout large organizations.

The second skill, fully participating in great teams, reflects the reality that healthcare is so complex, and the full episode of care is so broad, that no one can do a great job alone. We need great teams that can meet the needs of patients over time. And that means we need great team members. We have a lot of pickup teams in medicine; we need *real* teams, where everyone knows each other, everyone respects each other, and no one would ever want to let their teammates down.

The third skill, shaping the stories and memories of patients, reflects the insights in Daniel Kahneman's TED talk on memory and experience.[1]

Really excellent caregivers don't just show up and do a good job. They imagine the story that is being lived out by patients in front of them and do what they can to shape it so the memory patients have will be as good as possible. Everyone does that for patients whom they know or identify with; the critical skill needed to build trust in the times ahead is doing that for every patient.

My hope is that the goals described in this book and the skills outlined in Chapter 11 don't seem unattainable. Instead, my aim is to make them seem natural and possible, and reflective of the work that attracts people to healthcare. Over the last few years people in healthcare rose to the occasion over and over during periods of incredible duress, and my belief is that this demonstrates that the path I lay out makes sense and is possible. In fact, the ways in which healthcare has responded to crises have shown us the steps to take to become an HRO-NMW—a high-reliability organization, no matter what.

Notes

Introduction

1. Institute of Medicine, *To Err Is Human: Building a Safer Health System* (Washington, DC: The National Academies Press, 2000), https://doi.org/10.17226/9728.

2. Institute of Medicine, *Crossing the Quality Chasm: A New Health System for the 21st Century* (Washington, DC: The National Academies Press, 2001), https://doi.org/10.17226/10027.

3. Institute for Healthcare Improvement. "The IHI Triple Aim Initiative." n.d., http://www.ihi.org/Engage/Initiatives/Triple Aim/Pages/default.aspx.

4. Megan MacDavey, "System Redesign Part 1: Why It Matters," Peter & Elizabeth Tower Foundation, April 23, 2018, https://thetowerfoundation.org/2018/04/26/system-redesign-part-i-why-it-matters-html/.

5. A Jay Holmgren, Twitter post, September 15, 2021, 1:20 p.m., https://twitter.com/AJHolmgren/status/14381911145115 23844.

6. Gianrico Farrugia and Thomas H. Lee, "Cure, Connect, Transform: Three Mayo Clinic Strategy Components for Servant Leaders," *NEJM Catalyst*, July 9, 2020, https://catalyst.nejm.org/doi/full/10.1056/CAT.20.0416.

7. Deirdre E. Mylod and Thomas H. Lee, "Fixing Data Overload in Health Care," *Harvard Business Review*, March 16, 2022, https://hbr.org/2022/03/fixing-data-overload-in-health-care.

Chapter 1

1. Leon L. Haley and Thomas H. Lee, "Like a 100-Day Hurricane: Sustaining Months-Long Crisis Response," *NEJM Catalyst* 2, no. 3 (February 17, 2021), https://catalyst.nejm.org/doi/full/10.1056/CAT.20.0690.
2. Matthew Yglesias, "All Kinds of Bad Behavior Is on the Rise," Slow Boring, January 10, 2022, https://www.slowboring.com/p/all-kinds-of-bad-behavior-is-on-the?s=r.
3. Frances X. Frei and Anne Morriss, "Begin with Trust," *Harvard Business Review*, May–June, 2020, https://hbr. org/2020/05/begin-with-trust.
4. Frances X. Frei, "How to Build (and Rebuild) Trust," filmed April 2018 at TED2018, video, https://www.ted.com/talks/frances_frei_how_to_build_and_rebuild_trust?language=en.
5. Tejal Gandhi, "Lessons Learned from Restricted Visitation," *The Joint Commission*, January 12, 2022, https://www.jointcommission.org/resources/news-and-multimedia/blogs/improvement-insights/2022/01/lessons-learned-from-restricted-visitation/#.Yj9y9C-B02I.
6. Thomas H. Lee, Kevin G. Volpp, Vivian G. Cheung, and Victor J. Dzau, "Diversity and Inclusiveness in Health Care Leadership: Three Key Steps," *NEJM Catalyst*, June 7, 2021, https://catalyst.nejm.org/doi/full/10.1056/CAT.21.0166.
7. Holmgren, Twitter post, September 15, 2021.
8. Michael Karpman and Stephen Zuckerman, "The Uninsurance Rate Held Steady During the Pandemic as Public Coverage Increased," Urban Institute, August 18, 2021, https://www.urban.org/research/publication/uninsurance-rate-held-steady-during-pandemic-public-coverage-increased.
9. The Chartis Group, "Medicare Advantage Enrollment Continues to Surge in an Increasingly Complex and Competitive Landscape," *2022 Medicare Advantage Competitive Enrollment Report*, February 25, 2022, https://www.chartis.com/insights/medicare-advantage-enrollment-continues-surge-increasingly-complex-and-competitive.

Chapter 2

1. Nicholas Bloom, Raffaella Sadun, and John Van Reenen, "Does Management Matter in Healthcare?" *Hospital Organization and Productivity Conference*, October 2014, National Bureau of Economic Research, Cambridge, MA, https://www.ihf-fih.org/resources/pdf/Does_Management_Matter_in_Healthcare.pdf.
2. Thomas H. Lee, "Zoom Family Meeting," *New England Journal of Medicine* 384 (April 29, 2021): 1586–1587, https://www.nejm.org/doi/full/10.1056/NEJMp2035869.
3. Brigham and Women's Hospital, "Statement for Media Regarding Covid-19 Cluster," October 16, 2020, https://www.brighamandwomens.org/about-bwh/newsroom/press-releases-detail?id=3684.

4. Tejal K. Gandhi, Derek Feeley, and Dan Schummers, "Zero Harm in Health Care," *NEJM Catalyst* (March–April, 2020), https://catalyst.nejm.org/doi/full/10.1056/CAT.19.1137.

5. Karen M. Murphy, Jaewon Ryu, Allison Hess, Stephanie A. Gryboski, and Stanley I. Martin, "'Waiting for This Day Since March': Geisinger's Covid-19 Vaccine Program," *NEJM Catalyst*, December 22, 2020, https://catalyst.nejm.org/doi/10.1056/CAT.20.0683.

6. Stanley I. Martin, Allison Hess, and David K. Vawdrey, "Speed of Impact of Vaccination Campaign Within Geisinger's Workforce," *NEJM Catalyst*, March 26, 2021, https://catalyst.nejm.org/doi/10.1056/CAT.21.0105.

7. Jonathan Gleason, et al., "The Devastating Impact of Covid-19 on Individuals with Intellectual Disabilities in the United States," *NEJM Catalyst*, March 5, 2021, https://catalyst.nejm.org/doi/full/10.1056/CAT.21.0051.

8. Karthik Sivashanker and Tejal K. Gandhi, "Advancing Safety and Equity Together," *New England Journal of Medicine* 382 (January 23, 2020): 301–303, https://doi.org/10.1056/NEJMp1911700.

9. Jessica Dudley, Sarah McLaughlin, and Thomas H. Lee, "Why So Many Women Physicians Are Quitting." *Harvard Business Review*, January 19, 2022. https://hbr.org/2022/01/why-so-many-women-physicians-are-quitting.

10. Mirco Nacoti, et al., "At the Epicenter of the Covid-19 Pandemic and Humanitarian Crises in Italy: Changing Perspectives on Preparation and Mitigation," *NEJM Catalyst*, March 21, 2020, https://catalyst.nejm.org/doi/10.1056/CAT.20.0080.

11. Frederick P. Cerise, Brett Moran, Philip P. Huang, and Kavita P. Bhavan, "The Imperative for Integrating Public Health and Healthcare Delivery Systems." *NEJM Catalyst* 2, no. 4 (April 2021), https://doi.org/10.1056/CAT.20.0580.

12. Rahul Sharma and Thomas H. Lee, "Telemedicine Is Medicine: Training Medical Students on Virtual Visits," *NEJM Catalyst*, September 3, 2021, https://catalyst.nejm.org/doi/full/10.1056/CAT.21.0325.

13. Ceci Connolly and Connie Hwang, "Nonprofit Health Plans Launch Telehealth-First Options to Increase Access and Affordability," *NEJM Catalyst*, April 15, 2021, https://catalyst.nejm.org/doi/full/10.1056/CAT.21.0031.

14. Simin Gharib Lee, Alexander Blood, William Gordon, and Benjamin Scirica, "Disruptive and Sustaining Innovation in Telemedicine: A Strategic Roadmap," *NEJM Catalyst*, December 28, 2021, https://catalyst.nejm.org/doi/full/10.1056/CAT.21.0311.

15. Griffin Myers, Geoffrey Price, and Mike Pykosz, "A Report from the Covid Front Lines of Value-Based Primary Care," *NEJM Catalyst*, May 1, 2020, https://catalyst.nejm.org/doi/full/10.1056/CAT.20.0148.

16. Robert A. Phillips, Roberta L. Schwartz, H. Dirk Sostman, and Marc L. Boom, "Development and Expression of a High-Reliability Organization," *NEJM Catalyst*, November 10, 2021, https://catalyst.nejm.org/doi/full/10.1056/CAT.21.0314.

17. Min P. Kim, et al., "Health System Strategy to Safely Provide Surgical Care During the Covid-19 Pandemic," *NEJM Catalyst* 3, no. 2 (February 2022), https://doi.org/10.1056/CAT.21.0318.

Chapter 3

1. Daniel Kahneman, "The Riddle of Experience vs. Memory," TED 2010, https://www.ted.com/talks/daniel_kahneman_the_riddle_of_experience _vs_memory?language=en.
2. Chartis Group, "Medicare Advantage Enrollment Continues to Surge in an Increasingly Complex and Competitive Landscape," *2022 Medicare Advantage Competitive Enrollment Report*, February 25, 2022. https://www.chartis.com /insights/medicare-advantage-enrollment-continues-surge-increasingly -complex-and-competitive.

Chapter 4

1. Michael E. Porter, *Competitive Advantage: Creating and Sustaining Superior Performance* (New York: Free Press, 1985).
2. Eric C. Makhni, et al., "The Benefits of Capturing PROMs in the EMR," *NEJM Catalyst Innovations in Care Delivery* 2021 2, no. 8, August 2021, https://doi.org/10.1056/CAT.21.0134.
3. Stephen M. Shortell, "How 30 Percent Became the 'Tipping Point,'" *NEJM Catalyst*, August 8, 2016, https://catalyst.nejm.org/doi/full/10.1056/CAT .16.0780.

Chapter 5

1. Adam Grant, *Think Again: The Power of Knowing What You Don't Know* (New York: Viking, 2021), 45–47.
2. Grant, *Think Again*, 66–67.
3. Grant, *Think Again*, 72.
4. Amy Edmondson, "Building a Psychologically Safe Workplace," TEDxHSGE, May 5, 2014, https://www.youtube.com/watch?v=LhoLuui9gX8.
5. Barclay E. Berdan and Thomas H. Lee, "Covid-19 Learnings from the Ebola Crisis," *NEJM Catalyst*, January 26, 2022, https://catalyst.nejm.org/doi/full /10.1056/CAT.22.0035.
6. Berdan and Lee, "Covid-19 Learnings from the Ebola Crisis."
7. Michael E. Porter and Thomas H. Lee, "Integrated Practice Units: A Playbook for Healthcare Leaders," *NEJM Catalyst*, January 2021, https://doi .org/10.1056/CAT.20.0237.
8. Judd E. Hollander and Rahul Sharma, "The Availablists: Emergency Care Without the Emergency Department," *NEJM Catalyst*, December 21, 2021, https://catalyst.nejm.org/doi/full/10.1056/CAT.21.0310.
9. Robert A. Phillips, et al., "Development and Expression of a High-Reliability Organization," *NEJM Catalyst*, November 17, 2021, https://catalyst.nejm .org/doi/full/10.1056/CAT.21.0314.

10. Deirdre E. Mylod and Thomas H. Lee, "Fixing Data Overload in Health-care," *Harvard Business Review*, March 16, 2022, https://hbr.org/2022/03/fixing-data-overload-in-health-care.

Chapter 6

1. Kelli J. Swayden, Karen K. Anderson, Lynne M. Connelly, et al., "Effect of Sitting vs Standing on Perception of Provider Time at Bedside: A Pilot Study," *Patient Education and Counseling* 86:166–171, 2012, https://doi.org/10.1016/j.pec.2011.05.024.

2. Denisa Urban, Barbara K. Burian, Kripa Patel, et al., "Surgical Teams' Attitudes About Surgical Safety and the Surgical Safety Checklist at 10 Years: A Multinational Survey," *Annals of Surgery Open* 2: e075, September 2021, https://doi.org/10.1097/AS9.0000000000000075.

3. Amy Compton-Phillips, "No Stories Without Data, No Data Without Stories," *NEJM Catalyst*, October 18, 2017, https://catalyst.nejm.org/doi/full/10.1056/CAT.17.0364.

4. Senem Guney and Thomas H. Lee, "When Is Humor Helpful?" *Harvard Business Review*, November 17, 2021, https://hbr.org/2021/11/when-is-humor-helpful.

5. Mirco Nactoi, et al., "At the Epicenter of the Covid-19 Pandemic and Humanitarian Crises in Italy: Changing Perspectives on Preparation and Mitigation," *NEJM Catalyst*, March 21, 2020, https://catalyst.nejm.org/doi/10.1056/CAT.20.0080.

6. The National Patient Safety Foundation's Lucian Leape Institute, *Shining a Light: Safer Health Care Through Transparency* (Boston: National Patient Safety Foundation, 2015), https://psnet.ahrq.gov/issue/shining-light-safer-health-care-through-transparency.

7. Senem Guney, Zach Childers, and Thomas H. Lee, "Understanding Unhappy Patients Makes Hospitals Better for Everyone," *Harvard Business Review*, April 2, 2021, https://hbr.org/2021/04/understanding-unhappy-patients-makes-hospitals-better-for-everyone.

Chapter 7

1. Patrik Lindenfors, Andreas Wartel, and Johan Lind, "'Dunbar's Number' Deconstructed," *Biology Letters*, May 5, 2021, https://royalsocietypublishing.org/doi/10.1098/rsbl.2021.0158.

2. Ronald A. Williams and Thomas H. Lee, "What's the Performance Implication of a Nondiverse Leadership Team?," *NEJM Catalyst*, June 3, 2021, https://catalyst.nejm.org/doi/full/10.1056/CAT.21.0209.

3. Cleveland Clinic, "Empathy: The Human Connection to Patient Care," February 27, 2013, www.youtube.com/watch?v=cDDWvj_q-o8.

4. Melinda Ashton, "Getting Rid of Stupid Stuff," *New England Journal of Medicine* 379: 1789–1791, November 8, 2018, https://doi.org/10.1056/NEJMp1809698.

5. Michael J. Dowling, et al., "Covid-19 Crisis Response: First, Address the Safety and Well-Being of Your Team," *NEJM Catalyst*, December 2, 2020, https://catalyst.nejm.org/doi/full/10.1056/CAT.20.0544.

6. Kimani Paul-Emile, Alexander K. Smith, Bernard Lo, and Alicia Fernández, "Dealing with Racist Patients," *New England Journal of Medicine* 374: 708–711, February 25, 2016, https://doi.org/10.1056/NEJMp1514939.

7. WellSpan Health, "Patient Rights and Responsibilities," December 9, 2020, https://www.wellspan.org/patients-visitors/patient-guide/prepare-for-your-appointment/patient-rights-and-responsibilities/.

8. Amos Tversky and Daniel Kahneman, "Advances in Prospect Theory: Cumulative Representation of Uncertainty," *Journal of Risk and Uncertainty* 5: 297–323, October 1992, http://www.jstor.org/stable/41755005.

9. Hospital Consumer Assessment of Healthcare Providers and Systems, "HCAHPS Fact Sheet (CAHPS® Hospital Survey)," April 2022, https://hcahps online.org/globalassets/hcahps/facts/hcahps_fact_sheet_april_2022.pdf.

10. Kirk J. Brower, et al., "The Evolving Role of the Chief Wellness Officer in the Management of Crises by Healthcare Systems: Lessons from the Covid-19 Pandemic," *NEJM Catalyst Innovations in Care Delivery*, May 2021, https://doi.org/10.1056/CAT.20.0612.

Chapter 8

1. Agency for Healthcare Research and Quality, *National Healthcare Quality and Disparities Report Chartbook on Patient Safety, 2021* (Rockville, MD: AHRQ), Pub. No. 21-0012, February 2021, https://www.ahrq.gov/sites/default/files/wysiwyg/research/findings/nhqrdr/chartbooks/patientsafety/2019qdr-patient-safety-chartbook.pdf.

2. Lee A. Fleisher, Michelle Schreiber, Denise Cardo, and Arjun Srinivasan, "Health Care Safety During the Pandemic and Beyond—Building a System that Ensures Resilience," *New England Journal of Medicine* 386: 609–611, February 12, 2022, https://doi.org/10.1056/NEJMp2118285.

3. Tejal Gandhi, et al., "Zero Harm in Health Care," *NEJM Catalyst Innovations in Care Delivery* 1, no. 2, March–April 2020, https://doi.org/10.1056/CAT.19.1137.

4. Senem Guney, Chrissy Daniels, and Zach Childers, "Using AI to Understand the Patient Voice During the Covid-19 Pandemic," *NEJM Catalyst*, April 30, 2020, https://catalyst.nejm.org/doi/full/10.1056/CAT.20.0103.

Chapter 9

1. Karthik Sivashanker and Tejal K. Gandhi, "Advancing Safety and Equity Together," *New England Journal of Medicine* 382: 301–303, January 23, 2020, https://doi.org/10.1056/NEJMp1911700.

2. Tejal K. Gandhi, "Achieving Zero Inequity: Lessons Learned from Patient Safety," *NEJM Catalyst*, May 27, 2021, https://catalyst.nejm.org/doi/10.1056/CAT.21.0078.

3. National Steering Committee for Patient Safety, "Safer Together: A National Action Plan to Advance Patient Safety," (Boston, MA: Institute for Healthcare Improvement, 2020), http://www.ihi.org/Engage/Initiatives/National-Steering-Committee-Patient-Safety/Pages/National-Action-Plan-to-Advance-Patient-Safety.aspx.

4. Senem Guney and Tejal K. Gandhi, "Leveraging AI to Understand Care Experiences: Insights into Physician Communication Across Racial and Ethnic Groups," *NEJM Catalyst*, March 8, 2022, https://catalyst.nejm.org/doi/full/10.1056/CAT.21.0480.

5. Denitza P. Blagev, Nathan Barton, Colin K. Grissom, et al., "On the Journey Toward Health Equity: Data, Culture Change, and the First Step," *NEJM Catalyst*, July 2021, https://catalyst.nejm.org/doi/full/10.1056/CAT.21.0118.

6. David A. Ansell, Darlene Oliver-Hightower, Larry J. Goodman, and Omar B. Lateef, "Health Equity as a System Strategy: The Rush University Medical Center Framework," *NEJM Catalyst Innovations in Care Delivery*, May 2021, https://doi.org/10.1056/CAT.20.0674.

7. Lynne A. Chafetz, et al., "Building a Culture of Respect for People," *NEJM Catalyst Innovations in Care Delivery* 1, no. 6, November–December 2020, https://doi.org/10.1056/CAT.19.1110.

8. Frederick P. Cerise, Brett Moran, Philip P. Huang, and Karita P. Bhavan, "The Imperative for Integrating Public Health and Healthcare Delivery Systems," *NEJM Catalyst Innovations in Care Delivery* 2, no. 4, April 2021, https://doi.org/10.1056/CAT.20.0580.

Chapter 12

1. Daniel Kahneman, "The Riddle of Experience vs. Memory," TED 2010, https://www.ted.com/talks/daniel_kahneman_the_riddle_of_experience_vs_memory?language=en.

Index

About the Author

THOMAS H. LEE, MD, is Chief Medical Officer for Press Ganey Associates, Inc. He is an internist and cardiologist, practices primary care at Brigham and Women's Hospital in Boston, and is on the faculty of Harvard Medical School and the Harvard T. H. Chan School of Public Health. Prior to assuming his role at Press Ganey, he was Network President for Partners Healthcare System, the integrated delivery system founded by Brigham and Women's Hospital and Massachusetts General Hospital. He is a graduate of Harvard College, Cornell University Medical College, and Harvard School of Public Health.

Dr. Lee is a member of the boards of directors of Geisinger Health System, Health Leads, the Panel of Health Advisors of the Congressional Budget Office, and the editorial board of the *New England*

Journal of Medicine. He is the editor-in-chief of *NEJM Catalyst* and the author of *Chaos and Organization in Health Care* (MIT Press, 2009), *Eugene Braunwald and the Rise of Modern Medicine* (Harvard University Press, 2013), *An Epidemic of Empathy in Healthcare* (McGraw Hill, 2016), and *The Good Doctor* (McGraw Hill, 2020).